44 Soccer Defender Mistakes to Avoid

Mirsad Hasic

DEDICATION

I dedicate this book to my wife.

CONTENTS

ACKNOWLEDGMENTS

I would like to thank my family for their support.

Introduction

Hi, my name is Mirsad Hasic.

For those who may not be familiar with my work, allow me to explain a bit about my approach and style. The first thing I want to highlight is that I bring as much real-world information to the pages as I can.

Anyone can do a little research and write around a topic, but that's not my way. I like to get involved because you're involved, and so I need to know what it is that you'll be going through.

Everything you find in my books is researched thoroughly and experienced personally. I then pass on my findings and experiences, whenever appropriate, to you the reader. This is an approach to writing which helps me to connect better with my audience.

I, We, and You...

You will notice throughout this book how I write in the first person "I" quite a lot. This is deliberate. It is to make your journey more interesting and the reading experience less pressuring.

There are just too many coldly-written soccer guides on sale today, and that's one approach I make sure to avoid. The "I" accounts in this book are more likely to get your focus too. This is because you will relate to some of the things I write about on a more personal level.

I also use "we" on occasions as well. This is because I have been where you are at now, at least to some extent. This helps me to relate to what you're going through, meaning we're in this together. My personal approach lets you to pick up on similarities so much easier.

I also use the "you" approach because I'm addressing you, my reader, directly.

Inside "44 Soccer Defender Mistakes to Avoid" you will find a treasure-trove of useful information that you can put into practice right away.

This book covers not only the physical, but also the mental side of the soccer defending position. It explains in detail how the best of the best defenders avoid common mistakes and reach their greatness.

You will learn just what they did and how they did it. You will certainly be able to apply many of these things to your own game. The style of this book is one of "serious fun."

It's "serious" because I want you to succeed, and it's "fun" because without that there is no point. I am certain that these chapters will encourage you to read this book from cover to cover.

I am confident that you will want to get to work and apply many of the tips, advice and drills into your own game ASAP.

Understand the Offside Law in Soccer

In this intro section, we look at how to deal with offside situations. But there is something we need to do before we look at how to set the perfect offside trap. We first need to revise the official offside laws as set out by FIFA (The Fédération Internationale de Football Association).

The main offside law says:

"A player is in an offside position when this player is closer to the goal line of the opposite team than the last defender of that team in the same moment the passer plays the ball."

In simpler language, it is to prevent an attacking player from *waiting* for the ball close to the goal. Offside occurs when an attacking player goes behind the line of defenders *before* he has the ball in his possession.

It can all get a little confusing as you are probably aware. Don't worry. By the end of this section you will no longer wonder about the offside rule. Here is another simple explanation of it.

Let's say that the goal line is point A and his defender is standing at point C. Then, at the exact moment of passing the ball, any player standing at point B in between A and C is set to be offside.

This is the offside law in its simplest form. There are still some variations that you need to know about. I will explain these using various scenarios.

Scenario 1: Receiving the ball from the opponent while being in the offside.

This mostly happens when a defensive player, or this goalkeeper, mistakenly passes the ball to a player from the opposite team. In this case, the attacking player is not in an offside position.

It doesn't matter where he stands relative to the goal line, he cannot be offside in this situation. This is because it's clear that it's the defender/goalkeeper's fault. One of these guys has passed a wrong ball to his opponent and everyone knows it.

Scenario 2: Interfering.

The FIFA referee books states:

"Interfering with an opponent" means preventing an opponent from playing or being able to play the ball by clearly obstructing the opponent's line of vision or movement or challenging an opponent for the ball."

This second case causes a lot of problems for the referee. This is because it depends only on the referee's judgment. It's also because 90 percent of the time the referee's decision will lead to a disallowed goal. This means it's a major call and it has to be right.

In simpler terms, "Interfering" happens when a player who is in the offside position gets physically involved in a ball played by another player. That is, a teammate who is not in the offside.

It's quite difficult to understand this by just stating the rules. Because of this, I will illustrate it better by using six famous cases from the past few years.

Interfering case 1

The first case is infamous. There was a lot of buzz at the time of its happening, and a lot of anger too. It happened in a game between Portugal and Spain when Cristiano Ronaldo took the ball on the left flank. As he did this he made fun of the entire Spanish defense. Central defender, Gerard Pique, is still mocked by the infamous slide he made during that incident.

At this point, everything was fine for Ronaldo. The ball was heading toward the net without any opposition from the Spanish defense.

Ronaldo was ready to do his famous celebration until one of his teammates, Luís Nani, messed things up. Nani was in the offside at that moment, but he tried to score the goal himself nonetheless.

He hit the ball with his head instead of letting it enter the goal from Ronaldo's kick. The referee saw what had happened and canceled the goal.

Interfering case 2

The second incident happened in an English Premier League game. It was between Newcastle United and Manchester City.

In this incident, one of Newcastle's players, Cheick Tioté, sent a strong shot from outside the penalty area. So far so good, as the ball headed toward the goal.

Even though it went into the net, the referee canceled the goal. He did this because one of Newcastle United's players was in the offside position. From this offside position, he had blocked Manchester City's goalkeeper, Joe Hart, from seeing the ball.

Interfering case 3

The third incident happened in a game between Manchester City and Juventus. It was in the 2015/2016 Champions league.

In this play, one of Juve's players, Paul Pogba, sent a cross from inside City's penalty area. The ball headed toward two of his attacking teammates.

The first player, who was in the offside, ran towards the ball but failed to reach it in time. The second player, who was NOT in an offside position, also ran toward the ball.

He then managed to send an easy header into the goal. Despite the fact that Man City's keeper had zero chance of saving the ball, the referee canceled the goal.

He did this because of the movements of the first player, who had missed the ball.

The ref argued that the first player, who was offside at the time, made the keeper change his position. This is yet another case where an offside player had interfered with the game.

Case 3: When the ball returning to an offside player is unrelated to the offside trap:

An attacking player, let's call him player "A," from one team kicks the ball at the goal. That ball then rebounds back from the goalkeeper towards player "B." Player "B" is now in the offside position when he scores a goal. The goal will be disallowed ONLY if player "B" was in an offside position at the exact same moment that player "A" first attempted the goal.

Interfering Case 4

Here we look at the offside law in penalty kicks. In this first case, we take a situation where the ref allows the goal.

Sometimes, when a goalkeeper saves a penalty kick, it rebounds back to the penalty taker. The penalty taker will now be in the offside.

Despite his offside position, the law allows that player to play the ball again. If he scores, then that goal counts, despite the player being in the offside position.

In this second case, we look at a situation where the ref disallows the goal from a rebounded ball.

Let's assume the penalty shot hits the goal bars and rebounds back to the penalty taker. Let's also say the ball hits the bars before it touches the goalkeeper or any player from the opposite team.

In this case, the referee will call for an offside the moment the penalty taker touches or passes the ball, or shoots it toward the net for a second time.

The reason for this rule is because a ball hitting the bar cancels the penalty. So now the penalty taker is inside the penalty area where there is no defender between him and the goal line. And because the penalty is now cancelled, this puts the penalty shooter in the offside zone.

Interfering case 5

In case five we look at receiving the ball from a throw-in or a goal kick. Here we see why the offside trap doesn't apply. A lot of people know that a throw-in cancels the offside.

Not so many know about the goal kick though. Anytime a player passes a throw-in to a teammate who's in the offside, the game will keep going.

And when the opposition goalkeeper sends a goal kick toward one of his teammates, who's in an offside position, the game also continues. Both of these situations are ok and don't need referee's interference.

This means that you will have to mark all players receiving a throw-in regardless of their position. It also means that your team's defensive line should be beyond your opponent's last attacker.

In other words, you and your defensive teammates should be closer to the goal line than any player from the opposite team at the moment of receiving a goal kick.

If you leave an attacker behind you, and he receives the pass from the goal kick, you will be witness to an easy breakaway.

Interfering case 6

Here we take a look at when passing a penalty kick to a teammate is unrelated to the offside trap.

This is one situation that rarely happens in penalty kicks. But rarely doesn't mean never. There's nothing to prevent it from happening to you in the future, so you do need to be aware of it. A player who understands all the laws of soccer always has an upper hand.

This law states that any player who takes a penalty can pass the ball forward. This gives the penalty taker another option besides shooting straight at the goal. In other words, the rule allows him to pass the ball to a teammate.

Let's look at a situation to illustrate this better. The penalty taker could, if he wanted to, move the ball forward, even with a slight touch. As soon as he has done this, one of his teammates can run up from behind and strike the ball toward the net. If it goes in, the referee will allow the goal.

If the penalty taker passes the ball to the side, on the same horizontal line, or to the back of him, then the referee will cancel the penalty. He will then give an indirect free kick to the other team.

There is a famous incident where this happened. It was in a game between Ajax Amsterdam and Helmond Sport in 1982. It was in the Dutch league. Johan Cruyff, who we will talk about a lot in this book, turned a penalty into a 1-2 pass with one of his teammates.

What he did was pass the penalty kick to a teammate coming from behind him. This teammate then returned the ball back to Cruyff who then went on to score.

1. Not Knowing How to Set an Offside Trap That Works

OK, so we have looked at all possible cases for offside fouls. We will now look at how to successfully create an offside trap that works for you. To do this well you will have to follow these rules:

Picking the right moment: You can't put an attacker in the offside trap by running away from him after the ball is played. You have to move earlier than that. Any move you make to put a player in the offside should be before the ball leaves the passer's foot.

This is something that requires skill and experience. You must also be able to read the pass before it starts. It's crucial too that you can move quickly. That does not only apply to you, but your entire defensive line as well.

Distribute duties: You won't have time to look around and assess situations too much. This means you have to distribute duties among your defensive teammates.

When you play as a center back, you, and the other center back, do 90 percent of work. You two are the ones most likely to retreat back so that you can do a better job at defending your goal.

For you two center backs to set the perfect offside trap, you need to play smart. One of you should be responsible for two things. The first is to keep an eye on both the positioning and the movements of the last attacker from the opposite team.

In general, the attacker will position himself on the same line as you and your teammate. If he's not on the same line, he will only be one or two steps away from it at best. He does this because he wants to avoid you guys putting him in the offside.

Once you are confident that the opposition attacker has settled in his new position, then it's time to act. Now is the time for you to call on the other center back to step forward so as to set the perfect offside trap. It's important that you do this just before the pass takes place.

OK, so these are the things the first center back handles. Let's now look at the role of the second CB in these situations.

The other CB needs to watch out for, and meet, any other attackers coming up from behind. This may sound easy for the second CB since it's the only job he has to do, but it's not easy. It is in fact a sensitive and important responsibility.

Quite often there will be more than just one intruder to look out for. Most attacks don't only include a lone center forward. More often than not there will be many attacking midfielders.

There may even be a second striker trying to run through the opposite team's defensive. He does this in his attempt to get into a better position for the ball. So there can be a lot going on at any given time.

The question you might bet asking is this: How do you decide which CB calls for the offside trap and who deals with the other attackers.

The slower of the two center backs is the one who's responsible for calling the offside trap. This is important.

You play it like this to avoid any lag between the movements of the slower CB and his quicker defensive partner.

So it's necessary to give the slower of the two defenders the time he needs. He then has a chance to estimate his capabilities, as well as his speed.

If he makes it right on time, there's more chance that his faster teammate will make it right too.

Johan Cruyff has an intelligent quote about speed. His quote not only applies to football, but sports in general. He says this:

"What is speed? The sports press often confuses speed with insight. See, if I start running slightly earlier than someone else, I seem faster."

What if you are playing as a fullback?

As a full back, you shouldn't go deeper than your two center backs. The game is too quick for a center back to coordinate his movements with three other players at the same time. It will be both chaotic and catastrophic for him and his team.

To save the center back all the troubles, a fullback, playing on any of the two sides, should make sure he doesn't play deeper than his two center backs. What this means is that if you're standing on a line, the two center backs must be behind you.

Not in front of you, and not on the exact same line either, but always behind you. Doing this puts the responsibility of calling for the trap on their shoulders. It also allows you keep your focus on the guy coming right at you.

2. Not Being Good at Corners and Air Plays "Defensively"

A good defender is to be able to deal with corners, free kicks and different types of air plays. Having the ability to clear the penalty area from crossed balls gets him noticed.

In fact, it's the first thing talent scouts and coaches measure in a player. It is the best way to determine the ability of anyone wanting to play in the defensive lines.

The most expensive defensive players in the history of football are the best of the best in air plays. This includes both their defensive and offensive game. At the time of writing, the most expensive players are: David Luiz ($ 40 Millions) Thiago Silva, Rio Ferdinand ($ 50 Millions) and Alessandro Nesta (43 Millions).

How does one become great at headers?

To be great at headers you need to be good at five things. The first is that you must have an explosive jump. The second is a good intuition on where the ball will likely end up. The third thing is to consider the positions of all attacking players moving toward the ball.

That means the players behind you as well as in front. The fourth thing is that you have to be confident of being the first to reach the ball. And the fifth attribute you must have is the ability to send the ball to a safe place, well away from danger.

The Explosive Jump

If you have never seen Cristiano Ronaldo jumping or playing headers before, then I urge you to do so. You can learn a lot from his jumping and heading style.

The Complete Ron (as fans like to call Ronaldo) is currently one of the best jumpers and headers in European soccer. This is despite the fact that he's not that tall (Ronaldo is only 1.85 m).

Stature aside, Ronaldo's take-off and jumping style is much better than his taller peers. That includes those on both the attacking and the defensive lines.

It's not only his ability to jump higher than any giant defender marking him that makes Ronaldo so good.

It's also his ability to head the ball with the right power and in the right direction that makes him so special. And perhaps most impressive of all is that he doesn't need too much space to prepare for his jump.

Yes, the Real Madrid's star is impressive when playing high balls; that's for sure. But what's most impressive of all is that he wasn`t like this a few years ago. This is a skill he has developed from the ground up.

I can remember seeing him play for Sporting Lisbon. I can also remember him at Manchester United in the premier league.

Ronaldo was still good back then, but he wasn't the great jumper that he is today. He spent his years at Man United developing his game. He achieved 118 goals in 292 games before exploding in Madrid (321 goals in 307 games).

So the impressive jumps and headers that you see Ronaldo make today with Real Madrid are not the result of some natural talent. His ability came about as a result of working tirelessly on his skills.

Ronaldo got obsessed about enhancing his performance and took things to a whole new level. He even asked the famous athlete Usain Bolt, the fastest man on earth, to teach him how to run faster.

He also took lessons from professional NBA players. These guys taught him how to jump. They showed him how to extend his body to the max so that he could make explosive take-offs. With their help, Ronaldo was able to jump higher than those marking him.

Right now, Ronaldo is one of the best attacking players in the entire history of soccer. He has three Ballon D`ors and a 17 million EUR annual salary. The Ballon D`ors is an annual association football award given by FIFA. The award goes to the male player considered to have performed the best in the previous calendar year.

This shows you how working on yourself can make you great. Not all players are lucky to be born with natural talents. But even talent alone is useless without commitment and hard work. And many players become great because they don't ever give up on themselves, no matter what. If you want to become a great defender, understand that it all starts with the explosive jump.

Explosive jumps, or power jumps, will work miracles for you. I have seen players from both sides (defenders and attackers) score great goals from headers. And they often achieve this despite being shorter than those defenders marking them.

How to Improve Your Jump

Boosting your jumping ability all starts at the gym. This is because you need to exercise the muscles responsible for the jumping process. Those muscles include the abs and leg muscles, including the calves. You need to incorporate all the exercises below into your training routine. These are the ones which will help to develop all the right muscles. Work on these areas and you will achieve stronger, higher jumps on the field.

Jump Exercises

- **Abs crunches**: 4–6 sets, for 15-20 repetitions
- **Spiderman Plank Crunch**: 4–6 reps, 10 reps for each side.
- **Planks**: 3-4 sets, 1–2 minutes each.
- **Jump Squat**: 4-6 sets, 10–12 reps each and one minute's rest between each set.
- **Frog Jumps**: 4-6 sets, 10–12 reps each and one minute's rest between each set.
- **Squats**: High rep range, low to moderate weights.
- **Calves**: Do calf raises (seated and raised) as well as leg presses on the smith machine.

These are the exercises that will help you improve your vertical jump, thus enabling you to reach new heights. Having a good jump is only half the deal though. You still you need to know how to improve your headers and have them reach the net.

Judging Where the Ball Will End Up

Knowing where the ball is likely to end up requires a lot of experience. Experience is only something you can acquire over time. It is not something that you can get from a book.

A book can guide you and show you how best to gain your experience, but it's up to you to take action. Experience not only comes from practice but by observing too. How a player reads the game is something that can make or break him.

As I mentioned earlier, you have to start running before anyone else figures out where the ball will end up. This doesn't rely just on speed, but more on your ability to read the game. It also requires that you are familiar with your opponent's playing style.

Consider the Positions of All Attackers Around You

Before you decide what you will do with your header, there is something you must do. You must first know the positions of all the attackers around you. In many situations an attacker will sneak up from behind.

He then gets to hit the ball toward the near post before anyone spots him. You don't want this to happen to you so you have to determine the positions of your opponents relative to the ball.

Then, and only then, can you decide how to react. Maybe you will go for the ball or prepare yourself to block it after the opponent kicks it.

Whatever your decision is, the more you know about your surroundings, the better informed you will be.

Move Toward the ball

The first thing to do as you reach for the ball is to make sure your path is clear. That applies to players on both sides. The last thing you want is bodies around, restricting your movements.

The second thing you should do is to run over and meet the cross. If you stand around and wait for the ball to come to you, then you are likely to fail. The way to achieve these things is by your positioning.

You have to position yourself in a way that enables you to take one, two or even three steps to the front before jumping for the header.

This will allow you to muster all the power you need to head the ball. Anytime you jump for a cross from the standing still position, you limit yourself.

Being able to reach your greatest height gives you an immediate advantage over any attacker coming up from behind. Being first to the ball also means other players do not obstruct your efforts.

Send the Ball to the Safest Possible Place

When you play a header from a corner kick or a foul there is something you must never do. You must never send the ball toward any opponent facing the penalty area or standing on its edge.

If you do, they may get to start a fresh attack before your teammates have reorganized themselves.

Keep your header to the sides of the penalty area. Also play it high so that you force the ball to take longer before it reaches the ground.

This tactic gives you and your teammate's valuable extra seconds. It might not sound like much, but it is. A couple of extra seconds can give you enough time to prepare yourselves before the next attack.

And finally, avoid sending a header toward the center of the penalty area. Oftentimes, there will be a player from the opposite team hanging around there. This will likely be a stopper or a short striker.

They are opportunistic, just hoping and waiting for a chance to receive the ball. And if they do, they get to smash it right toward the net. So make things harder for them and send your headers toward the right or left edge of this area.

3. You Take Easy Yellow Cards

As a defender you are "card prone" by nature. Whenever you can, always save your first yellow card for the end of the game.

Any yellow card you take in the first 40 or 50 minutes will have a negative effect on your performance. It will make you more cautious and prevent you from going after the ball with your full capacity and strength.

An early yellow card puts you at a huge disadvantage. It gives your opponents the chance to keep all their balls and concentrate a decent percentage of their attacks on your side of defense.

This is because they now know you have to tame your game down a notch or two if you're to avoid another yellow card.

It also means they have a better chance to reach your goal. They understand that you won't be able to slide or make aggressive tackles against them.

And if you do end up with another yellow card, you give the rival side a chance to outnumber your team. That then creates even more danger for your side.

The way to steer clear of this problem is to avoid any unwanted tackles or fouls at the beginning of the game. This includes the following:

Aggressive Tackles in "Safe" Areas

Examples of this can be when tackling an opponent in his own half. Another is to tackle the opponent on both sides of the center line. Also, avoid aggressive tackles on your opponents anywhere on the field where you have more than one player covering you.

Note too that you should never ever tackle a player from behind, unless you have a solid reason to do so. If someone tricks you into making this horrible mistake the referee will send you off with a direct red card.

Since the law is so strict in these cases, many refs tend to send a player off automatically. He will do this even if you managed to touch the ball, which is the only reason that cancels the foul.

Taking off Your T-Shirt After Scoring a Goal

You might have seen this happen a few times in the past. A player scores a goal and celebrates by taking off his t-shirt and waving it around in triumph.

He then gets a yellow card for his misbehavior. Then, a few minutes later, he makes a foul. He then receives his second yellow card and the referee sends him off the field.

I have seen a ref send a player off directly after celebrating with the t-shirt waving. This happened because the player forgot he had a previous yellow card from earlier in the game.

He kept begging the referee not to send him off, but the ref was having none of it. The law is the law, and taking off your clothes will get you booked.

Wasting Time When Playing a Throw-in or an Indirect Free Kick

This happens mostly with goalkeepers when their team is leading the score. What happens is that they try to waste a few seconds of playing time by delaying a goal kick or an indirect free kick. This tactic can involve defenders too, but it can also result in yellow cards. Let's look at some scenarios.

The first happens when your keeper tries to waste some time by asking you to take the free kick instead of him. Take heed! If you take too long playing the ball, you'll be guilty of wasting time. If the referee thinks this is the case, he will give you a yellow card.

The second case is when you take too much time before playing a throw-in. Again, if the referee thinks you're wasting time he will warn you. If the playing atmosphere is already tense, he may just book you.

Touching the Ball with Your Hands in a Safe Place

The 2006 World Cup was in Germany. There was one game remembered in that World Cup, for all the wrong reasons. It was when Portugal and The Netherlands played against each other in the quarter final.

They called that game "The Battle of Nuremberg." This was because the Russian referee, Valentin Ivanov, showed a total of 16 yellow cards and 4 red cards. He gave these out to 12 different players from the two teams. That's not what you might call the best behaved of games!

One of those four red cards went to Portugal's player, Costinha. He actually received two consecutive yellow cards. The first was an early unwanted tackle at the thirtieth minute. The second was in the last minute of the first half.

It was after he attempted to touch a ball with his hand in the center of the field. In fact, the ball was heading toward the Portuguese half where there were eight Portuguese waiting for it and only two Dutch attackers.

Acting / Simulation

The other cause of an unwanted yellow card is when you pretend or simulate that an opponent has hit you. You do this in an attempt to convince the referee of the wrongdoing. Your hope is that the ref will send the player off or at least give him a yellow card.

In some cases the referee will be close enough to catch your sneaky trick. When this happens, you simulation attempt will backfire and it will be you who receives a yellow card. This humiliation will probably have a negative effect on the way you play the rest of the game too.

Being Simulated On

During the battle of Nuremberg just mentioned, the Netherland's defender, Khaled Boulahrouz, received his second yellow card after being simulated on by Portugal's player, Luis Figo.

It happened when Figo was running behind Boulahrouz, whose hand accidentally touched the Portuguese's face. Figo then threw himself to the ground, making it look as though he had been whacked. He hadn't, of course. He was simply taking advantage of the situation. It worked too, and the referee sent the Dutch player off the field with a second yellow card.

Grabbing an Attacker's T-Shirt from Behind

One of the easiest ways to get an unwanted yellow card is to grab a player's t-shirt from the back. You're even more likely to get a card when the play is far away from your goal and shows no threat to your team.

Of course, there will be times when you have to stop an attacker using whatever means are possible. A little misbehavior is sometimes necessary to prevent him from scoring or threatening your goal.

An example might be when there is a counter attack and the opponents in the area outnumber you. Even so, this kind of behavior should always be the exception and never the rule. In other words, use it in situations that call for desperate measures.

Defender will often find themselves in situations where they are nutmegged or outrun. They may feel humiliated by skilled, fast attackers.

In these circumstances it's tempting to lose one's cool by grabbing an attacker's t-shirt. Such moments of madness are not untypical when the pressure is on.

But it's important to understand that spontaneous outbursts like these rarely help a situation. They will always happen though; such is the nature of the game. As I pointed out earlier, defenders in particular are card prone.

This is why you have to learn how to control your emotions when things get rough. You need to find the balance where you can stop an attack with proportional force. The idea is to be borderline tough. All that means is that you get to go in hard but with a minimal risk of getting a card.

Defender's will always be card-prone, that will never change. Your only real defense is to play smart and know your options at any given time. This is something that can only come about with experience.

4. Not Able to Overcome a Lack in Physical Strength

One defender on this list is the Arsenal and Germany defender, Per Mertesacker (1.98 m).

It's common for defenders to be tall and strong. Those who are not may find that some people, including coaches, suggest that playing on the back line is not for them. They may even tell them to try another position or another sport altogether. You might have heard that a good defender is judged only by his physical strength. This is not so. It's a myth that needs debunking.

There are many examples of elite defenders of all statures and strengths who have mastered their game. And no, not all these guys have outstanding physical strength. There are also many examples of defenders who are tall like giants, and look as tough as beasts.

Yet appearances can be deceptive at times. Despite their stature and strength, they are not so good at defending. As I say, looks can be deceptive. It's like that wise old adage says: "Never judge a book by its cover."

Let's now look at each of these in turn, starting with the guys who seem to fit the bill because of their build.

Even Iversen

I will start with the tallest defender of all times. This is a player called Even Iversen. He is 6ft 8in (2.03 m). Yet despite his size, he wasn't able to make a decent career for himself in European soccer.

Per Mertesacker

Mertesacker doesn't make it to the list of the world's best defenders either. This is despite being a World Cup winner with Germany (he was a substitute). He was also Arsenal's captain. In fact, he won two consecutive FA cups with the English team.

The problem with Mertesacker is that he loses most of his quality whenever he teams up with a slow partner. Two seasons before he joined Arsenal (season 2010- 2011), he created a lot of problems.

In fact, he almost caused his team at the time, Werder Bremen, to relegate to Germany's league two. This was after a bad performance from him that created a lot of upset for the team.

To be fair to Mertesacker, he didn't play that bad compared to his teammates. His main weakness was his inability to play or team up with any defensive partner who lacked the speed to cover up for his own lack of pace.

In 2010, Mertesacker's main defensive partner in Werder Bremen got seriously injured. This resulted in him playing the entire season next to another giant. This guy, like Mertesacker, also needed someone to cover after him. The result was disastrous for his team. They finished the season in thirteenth place out of eighteen teams in the Bundesliga. The year before that they had finished in third place.

Even after moving to Arsenal, Mertesacker's performance had its bad moments. In fact, it declined anytime his fast defensive partner, Lauren Koscielny, missed a game because of an injury or a ban.

OK, let's now take a look at a couple of examples of great defenders who are anything but big, strong giants.

Lauren Koscielny

It's because of defenders like the quick and tiny Lauren Koscielny that I wrote this chapter. He is one of the most talented defenders in soccer today. And this is despite him not having a solid, strong body and despite being only 1.86 m tall.

Koscielny and Thiago Silva (1.83 m) are both special. They are the type of defenders who can compensate for their lack in strength and stature. They do this with their smart moves and aggressive, well-timed tackles.

Both players also have an uncanny ability to read the game. They know how to position themselves just right. This gives them a huge advantage over any attacker playing against them.

Koscielny has scored a total of 11 goals for Arsenal since he joined the team in 2010. Silva has scored 30 goals in his career. Both of them have been chosen to be part of their league's dream team, and quite rightly so.

What this all tells us is that it's more about the style of the defender that matters. Any lack in physical features does not mean a lack in ability to excel in this role. In other words, it doesn't matter if you are not as strong as your peers.

What matters is that you never allow anyone to convince you that you're not up to the mark because of some lack in strength and/or stature. You have to build on what you do have rather than worry about what you don't.

5. Not Playing Deep in the Back to Cover Any Lack of Speed

The sweeper, known in Italy as the Libero, is the closest defender to the goalkeeper. He is also the last defender to play behind the defensive line. The sweeper's job is to move around freely.

The word libero literally means "free" in Italian. So the sweeper is behind the defensive line and sweeps away all the balls that penetrate through.

This may include through passes and long lobs. He is also responsible for getting rid of any shots that rebound off the goalkeeper.

The sweeper also has another role, which is to provide safety and deep coverage for his teammates. The sweeper stays behind so that he can back up his team players and balance the play.

The sweeper's job rarely depends on speed. It relies more on how well he positions himself inside the penalty area, and how good he is at reading the game.

That means being able to predict where the next pass will head and who will receive it. A talented sweeper also has good passing skills, especially with long balls.

In many situations, the sweeper is the first player of his team to intercept or receive the ball. This means he must be ready and capable of distributing fast passes among his teammates.

It also means he must be able to send long passes toward the opposite side of the field. This allows him to create effective counter attacks.

You may have heard people talk about how the sweeper's role in modern soccer is dead. This is not quite true.

It is a fact that only the smallest of teams and old fashioned coaches still use a sweeper in their games. Why? Because it can kill the play and affect the team's attacking capabilities. Some say that the beauty of the game is gone when sweepers sweep.

Let's look at this a little closer, using the Greek side to illustrate. They were the champions of the 2004 Euro played in Portugal. They won against France (Zidane), and then against Portugal (Figo and Ronaldo) in the quarter final and then the final.

But despite these victories, all the Greek games were completely boring. In fact, they ended with only one goal difference for each game they won. This was due to the Italian defensive techniques applied by Greece's coach, Otto Rehhagel. He was the only coach to play using a real sweeper.

In the mid-1990s the big teams started to abandon all strategies and game plans that required having a real sweeper on the field (like the Catennacio Italiano playing style). They finally realized that it undermines their ability to perform to best effect.

This doesn't mean that the sweeper role is gone from modern soccer. The big teams still use sweepers, but in a more hidden, less obvious way.

More than 90 percent of all teams now, in Europe's top five leagues, no longer play with obvious sweepers. This includes the English, Spanish, German, Italian and the Dutch leagues.

This is because no side these days uses five players in defense. Having an "obvious" sweeper also disrupts a team's ability to set successful offside traps.

Some big teams, however, will give the sweeper's role to their goalkeeper. That's providing he has the abilities and the skills to do the job.

Manuel Neuer of Germany and Bayern Munich, and Ter Steigen of Barcelona, are great examples of goalie sweepers.

Other times, the sweeper role goes to the slowest and the most experienced of the two center backs. Their job is to sweep the penalty area and then leave the sweeping role on the two flanks for the left and right backs.

How this works is that the slowest center back retreats behind his faster partner. This allows him to sweep up after him. It also lets him stay near his own area of work, which is inside the penalty area.

If a defender lacks speed because of his age, or because of his physical composition, all is not lost. He can still work at improving his leadership skills.

With a good awareness of his position, and an ability to read the game well, he gets to retreat a little. By doing this he can play as a center back and sweeper at the same time.

Do you ever feel that you don't have enough speed to support yourself when playing on the back line? If so, then find yourself a new role and start to improve your other skills. Look at ways to progress your leadership and communication skills.

Develop what you do have and focus on those areas. Once you do this, you will be able to jump over your weak points easy enough. You just need to be open to new ideas and possibilities, and then start searching for solutions.

6. Not Knowing When to Use Your Hands to Clear Away the Ball

Understand that it is generally unwise for a defensive player to use any of his hands to deflect a ball away from the goal.

For example, if an attacker gets past your goalie and shoots at an empty goal, don't try to stop the ball with your hands. If you, the defender, use your hands to save the ball, you will get a red card.

A penalty will also be given against your team. If the attacker still manages to score, despite your handball, your side will then be one goal behind and one player down. As you can see, using your hands is NOT a risk worth taking.

However, there is an exception to this general rule. Let's say the same situation happens just a few minutes before the game ends. And let's also say your team is winning.

In this situation, it might be worth stopping the ball with your hands. It is especially worth doing if that goal would result in an equalizer so close to the end of the game.

You see, using your hand in this situation is an act of preserving the score. There's always a chance that the other side will miss the penalty too.

And your team will have to spend the remaining minutes defending anyway. So it shouldn't matter too much if they defend with nine field players rather than ten. After all, it's only for the final moments of the game.

This exact situation happened in 2010. It was during the South African World Cup when Uruguay was tying with Ghana. It was a goal for each side and only a minute away before the inevitable penalty shootout.

So up till now it was still uncertain who would move to the semifinal and meet The Netherlands. Ghana then suddenly had a serious chance to score a last minute killer.

One of their players sent a powerful header toward Uruguay's goal. The Uruguayan keeper failed to stop the ball and it continued on toward the goal.

Just as the ball was about to reach the goalmouth, Uruguay`s attacker, Luis Suarez, used both his hands to stop it before it crossed the goal line.

The predicable consequences of this saw Suarez sent off and Ghana awarded a last minute penalty. What happened next is just what Suarez had hoped would happen.

The ball hit the crossbar and so the score remained the same. A few minutes later, as they moved to the shootout, the Ghanaian players were already feeling down. The previous failed penalty had dampened their spirits, as failed penalties tend to do.

This meant they were not entering the penalty shootout with as much confidence as they might have done otherwise. In fact, they were behaving as if they had already lost. This was great news for Uruguay, who then went on to win the shootout with the final score ending at 4-2 to them.

That illegal save made by Suarez was a game changer in this situation. There are those who support and call for "clean soccer" but who really cares when it's crunch time. That save helped his team reach the semifinal in one of the most prestigious competitions in soccer.

His save also made him a national hero with his country folks. He didn't care what others would say about his bad tactic, not in this situation. All he could think about was what all competitive soccer players think about, and that is winning.

7. Not Paying Enough Attention to the Player You Mark

What we are going to look at in this chapter doesn't in any way oppose to what I have mentioned before. That is, the importance of effective contribution and communication with your teammates. This is the only way to cover any holes in your defensive plan and play well as a unit.

However, there are some defensive players who put too much time into communicating. These are the guys whose eyes are constantly moving all around the field. They seem to be communicating with everyone. This is not as good as it sounds.

Too much communication can, and quiet often does, result is a loss of attention where it's needed most. Trying to be all things at all times to all people has its consequences.

It can mean that you forget what's most important to you, and that is the one player you should be marking.

Many goals that materialize are nothing but mistakes translated into goals. A mistake can be failing to take a proper dive (a goalkeeping mistake). It can also be losing the ball under pressure (a midfielder's mistake).

Then there's failing to finish an attack or making a wrong pass that leads to a counter attack (a striker`s mistake). And in our case here, failing to keep the ball away from the attacker you are marking (a defender's mistake).

Even if the player with the ball is as skilled as Messi or Ronaldo, a goal will always come about as the result of a single mistake made by one or more team members.

The golden rule here is to always keep your attacker in front of your eyes. Always be ready for any of his sudden moves.

Whenever you can, study these players before the game. Knowing something about their style of play before a game begins will put you at a huge advantage on the field.

If everyone on the defensive line sticks to the attacker he's responsible for, 100 percent of the time, guess what happens. You get to cut out 90 percent of the danger and boost your chances of having a clean sheet throughout the game.

So yes, keep an eye on the broader game at all times. But don't get so involved in what everyone else is doing to the point where you lose focus on what you're supposed to be doing. Your primary focus is to take care of the one you're marking.

8. Unable to Avoid Easy Own Goals

Most own goals are usually the result of one of three things. I'm talking about the regular type here, and not the crazy own-goals you find on YouTube.

Ball deflection is one of the main reasons for own goals. Another is a wrong slide. And the third is not considering the goalkeeper's position when sending the ball back to him.

OK, let's look at each of these one at a time.

Ball Deflection

There are times when you don't have full control over these kinds of balls. Quite often the ball is traveling too fast to do anything controlled and thoughtful with.

Still, there are two mistakes that many defenders make when trying to protect their goal by deflecting the ball with their legs or heads.

The first of these mistakes is to deflect the ball sideways instead of sending it to the front, out into the field. It sounds confusing, I know, but you will understand better in a moment.

When you try to save your goal from a strong shot, the safest place to send your deflected ball is to the front of you. Consider yourself facing a shot with your back facing the penalty area.

There is no chance that ball will deflect toward your goal if it deflects off you in this way. Many times the defender thinks it's safe to deflect the ball to his right or his left side.

He then realizes that the shot he thought he was about to save has caught him and his goalkeeper off guard.

It may go straight toward his goal. Its path is just too unpredictable this way. So the safest option here is to always keep the ball directed in a vertical direction, in front of you. Directing it in a horizontal direction is just asking for trouble.

The second mistake defenders make in such situations is not to meet the ball with enough force. The result of that can leave you exposed to danger. So always try to deflect the ball with as much force as you can muster.

This way, even if the ball reaches an opponent he will still have a hard job getting it under immediate control. That gives you, your teammates, and your goalie, more time to reorganize yourselves.

Always keep in mind that it doesn't take too much energy to deflect the ball toward your goal line. But it does need enormous energy to send it far away.

A Wrong Slide

The second reason for a team conceding an own goal is with a wrong slide. This happens when a defensive player slides to intercept a pass or a low cross inside the penalty box.

These actions are usually taken close to the actual goal. And instead of sending the ball far away from the goal, the defender does the opposite. He scores against his own team. Whoops!

The best way to avoid this mistake is to always slide in a diagonal direction. If you slide in a vertical direction, toward the goal area, you are gambling with the outcome.

The foot used to clear the ball, as well as your lower body, should be at an angle. In other words, you are pointing anywhere but the goal area. This is the only way to avoid risking an own goal with a slide tackle.

The Escobar Case

The simple advice you're reading right now could have saved the life of the Colombian defender, Andrés Escobar. I mean that in the literal sense. Escobar was playing for his country in the group stage against USA in the 1994 World Cup.

The game looked easy for the Colombians. After all, they had three of the most talented players in the world at that time. They were Carlos Valderrama, Faustino Asprilla and Escobar. Andrés Escobar was all set to join AC Milan right after the world cup.

Colombia had lost its first game against Romania so it had to win the game against the Americans. Despite the pressure, the Colombian players showed no signs of stress after the game got underway.

This all changed though, somewhere around the middle of the first half. It was when Escobar was trying to intercept a low cross with a slide tackle.

Unlucky for him, that slide went all wrong and he scored an own goal. The USA maintained their lead of 1-0 throughout the game. Then, before the final whistle they scored, ending with a 2-0 win.

Now that Colombia was out of the World Cup, Escobar flew back to his own country. What happened next was a tragedy.

He was outside a local bar where he got shot six times in the chest by an angry fan. This fatal incident happened just a few weeks before his wedding was due to take place.

When you watch the own-goal that Escobar scored, it is easy to see why it happened. You can see that the whole problem was in the way he slid and not in the slide itself. His lower body was pointing straight at his goal area.

The mistake was not the decision to slide. Under the circumstances, that was his only option. Where he blundered was in the way he positioned his body to clear the ball. It was, in fact, an avoidable own goal.

Not Considering the Keeper's Position When Making a Pass to Him

The third and the rarest type of own goal happens when the defensive player sends a pass toward his goal. This is usually, but not always, the mistake made by a center back.

What he does is send the ball to the goal using too much power. Or he might just make the pass without considering the keeper's position first. It can also be a combination of these two things.

Whenever you send the ball back to the keeper, it's important to keep any unnecessary pressure off him. Whatever you do, never pass the ball to your goalie before checking the area around the two of you is safe.

Too many mistakes occur when the defender does not focus. These mistakes also happen when there's a lack of communication between defender and keeper. Any pass made to the goalie that lacks accuracy, for whatever reason, is heading for disaster.

So what do I mean by an "inaccurate pass?" Well, this could be a pass that is either too strong or too weak (short) for the keeper to reach. Imagine that, a weak pass that a nearby opponent suddenly steals and shoots into your goal.

Or an overly strong pass that is just too powerful for the goalie to stop. Although these things are not that common, they do still happen nonetheless.

Here are some things that you always need to be mindful of when passing the ball back to the keeper.

1. Pass the ball outside of the goal area.

This simple strategy means you avoid own goals when passing the ball to the keeper. The goalie is also in a better position to then kick the ball with enough power and accuracy if he decides to send it over to the opposite side of the field. He also has more space and flexibility if he wants to start a counter attack.

Sometimes, the defender isn't paying enough attention when he passes the ball to his goalie. It is never a good idea to assume anything in these situations.

In other words, never believe the goalie knows that you're about to pass him the ball unless you have concurred. You must always know that he is ready for you 100 percent. If he's not, even the softest of shots can end up in his net.

I can recall one incident where this happened. It was in the English second division. The game was between Wolverhampton Wanderers and Bristol City. The Wolves' goalkeeper passed a goal kick toward his center back.

This poor guy then panicked when he realized there was an attacker right behind him. You can probably guess what happened next. He kicked a strong ball back toward the center of his own goal.

The goalkeeper, who can't use his hands in these situations, tried to stop the ball with his feet. He failed, thus letting the ball enter his goal.

Things might have turned out quite different if the defender was aware of the player behind him. He would have also fared better if he just kept a level head and thought about his options for a moment.

Sending the ball anywhere other than to his own goal, with a hard kick, would have been preferable. Hindsight is indeed a wonderful thing!

Always remember that as a defender, your main job is to keep balls away from your goal. So the further your passes are from your keeper and his goal line, the less danger you put your team in.

2. Pass the ball with suitable force.

Help the keeper receive the ball with ease and avoid shooting at him. By that I mean don't kick the ball, just pass it. There is a distinct difference.

Also, and whenever possible, try to make most passes to your goalkeeper using your head, instead of your foot.

This will allow your goalie to use his hands to catch the ball instead of forcing him to save it with his feet and legs. This way, he also has a better chance to create a more accurate counter attack.

This is because most goalkeepers find it easier and more accurate to direct the ball using a punt. It's certainly easier than kicking it straight from the ground.

3. Avoid giving the ball to the keeper when surrounded by opponents.

Only pass the ball to the keeper as your last option, when you feel pressured. If the keeper is far away from you and has nobody around him, then you are obviously freer to pass him the ball if you need to. For all other situations, think carefully before you bring the goalie into your game.

9. Not Being Good at Tackling

If you want to learn everything there is to know about good tackling, start to observe the greats. I recommend you watch and track four players in particular. The first two are legendary defenders.

The last two are currently the best in the world today and play in the defensive midfielder role. OK, let's take a look at each of these guys in turn. You will soon get to understand why I have picked them out.

The first two players are AC Milan's legendary couple. One is Alessandro Nesta and the other Paulo Maldine. The current stars in the world of soccer are Nemanja Matić and Francis Coquelin. Matić is one of best three defensive midfielders in European soccer.

As for Coquelin, he made more successful tackles and interceptions than any other player in Europe's top five soccer leagues. Most impressive of all is that he made them in one half of the 2014/2015 season.

These four players have four special qualities. These are essential for any defender to make what I call "the perfect tackle." Those qualities by order are: focus, aggression, bravery and anticipation.

1. Focus

The first skill is to fix your eyes on the ball and keep them firmly on it. By that I mean fix your eyes only on the ball, not on the movement of the player's legs or his body.

2. Aggression

The second skill here is aggression. By aggression I mean willing to perform a hard tackle whenever necessary. You need to be aggressive regardless of the other player's size or skills. You must not care about getting injured or humiliated. You must be 100 percent determined and confident of success. You must remove all thoughts of NOT being able to reach the ball from your head.

Aggression is something that relates back to mindset. It's how you perceive yourself. It's not a case of is there aggression within you, it's more a case of can you let it out when you need it.

Aggression will force you to go for every ball, every pass and every cross. It will let you take advantage of every mistake and erratic ball that comes into play. Only aggression and a strong work ethic will set you apart from your peers. It will perceive you as a formidable force on the soccer field.

It's important to put aggression into perspective. Many people think of aggression as feelings of anger or antipathy. They connect it with hostile or violent behavior. This is actually "uncontrolled aggression" and has no place on the soccer field.

What you need is "controlled aggression." It means you have a readiness to attack or confront with force and determination. But you do this in a controlled, yet forceful way. Just know that there is no time for good manners or hesitation on the soccer field.

3. Anticipation

The third skill is to have the ability to anticipate situations. You need to learn where the ball will likely go next. In many situations you will have to first predict where the ball will go before deciding to slide. This is especially important when intercepting crosses played low on the ground.

4. Bravery

Bravery will see you playing without fear and caution. And the braver you are the more confident you become in your ability as a defender. A great defender has good mental and physical toughness.

Note that being fearless is not the same as being careless. It means you have the courage to go into tough situations, but you also know when not to. Sometimes, the brave thing to do is to hold back, even when you would sooner get stuck in.

This is something that will develop with experience. The question you need to ask yourself now is whether you're as brave as you could be when playing in tough games. Note that developing bravery is more to do with psychology than physical ability.

Choosing the Perfect Launch Point

Before making any tackle you need to consider the right position from where to launch your slide, or other tackle.

Again, this is something that you will intuitively know what to do as you become more experienced. Choosing your launch point is a sensitive decision. It is something you need to do quickly yet with careful thought. If you slide too early and fail to make it to the ball, you then leave behind an empty space.

Any attacker will then be free to advance through that opening. Imagine if you're the last of your defenders and you botch the tackle.

Failing to reach the ball in this situation will result in a one-to-one confrontation between the attacker and your goalkeeper. This is something that will most likely end with a goal scored against your team.

10. Not Warming Up Well

The quality of your warmup affects the quality of your tackles.

Many times, the lack of proper warming up can affect your ability to stretch your legs fully. This will have an obvious negative impact on how you perform a tackle.

Even if you are young and supple, that doesn't mean you can skip a warm up before a practice or game. Warmups are necessary and not just done for the sake of it. Those who miss or skimp on warmups always pay a price. Let's now look at why it is so important to warm up.

1. It prevents injuries.
2. It prepares your physical condition.

Put another way, warming up prepares your body for action. It gets you to a level of flexibility that allows your body to handle different game requirements from the start.

Failure to warm up will mean you're not ready to handle fast, aggressive attacks during the first few seconds or minutes of the game. In other words, you're not in the best physical condition to react as well as you would like to.

A typical warming up routine should include the following:

Stretches

Begin with 2–4 minutes of light jogging. This warms up your joints by improving blood flow. This alone decreases the chances of getting injured.

After the light jog, perform 20 seconds of stretching for each of your major muscles. Those are the quads, hamstrings, calf, upper body, neck and shoulders. Don`t stretch to the point where you become fatigued or your muscles ache.

Stick to the 20 seconds for each muscle, no more. Accompany this with three sets of light jumping (20 seconds each). Once done, you're good to then start warming up with the ball.

Preparing for Different Plays

Now it's time to start practicing headers, slides and crosses from different places and at different speeds. Also take shots at the goal from different angles.

What you're doing here is getting yourself familiar with the game so that you are well-prepared for when it starts.

As you can see, there's not much to a standard warm-up. Failure to warm up though can, and often does, have a negative effect on your ability to play well in those early minutes of the game. Skipping a warm up is also the cause of many unnecessary injuries.

Imagine that, skipping a short warm up session resulting in unnecessary pain and discomfort. Worst still is that it could potentially see you taking months off the field to recover.

11. Poor Communication with Teammates

It doesn't always matter if there's a lack of strong communication between the midfield players. It's the same with attackers too.

Some teams even have successful players who can't stand each other, let alone communicate. Zlatan Ibrahimovich and Edison Cavani in Paris Saint-Germain are two examples of this.

This lack of communication is not such a problem whenever we move toward the front line of any soccer team.

This does not apply to back line though. It is crucial that the four, five or six guys playing at the back have excellent communication at all times.

This includes the goalkeeper. They must always maintain excellent communication and coordination between themselves.

As a defensive soccer player good communication between you and your goalkeeper is crucial. Both of you should be on the same page for almost every move and every attack against your team. Let's look at this in more detail.

Corners and Crosses

You and your keeper should talk about who will go out for the ball and who will stick to his position. In corner kicks, you have to communicate with your goalie to make sure no opponent restricts his movements. The goalie must always have a clear path whenever he leaves his goal to go after the ball.

You also have to listen to your goalkeeper. After all, he is the one with the best view of things. The goalie is in the best position to point out any uncovered players.

The keeper's job is to notify his teammates of any player coming in from behind to meet the corner kick. Your job is to listen to him and then mark that player.

Finally, there may be times when you choose to stand on the goal line in corners or free kicks. In these situations you'll have to communicate well with your keeper.

He will know the best position for you to take. The goalie always knows best when it comes to providing your team with the coverage it needs, and without restricting his movements.

Free Kicks

A goalkeeper should communicate with his teammates when setting up his defensive wall. This applies to both direct and indirect free kicks.

This communication is important for all concerned. The aim here is to block all possible shooting opportunities for the one taking the free kick.

A well-positioned wall also helps the keeper to maintain a good view for the ball. Any bad positioning by any team member standing in the wall can have dire consequences.

Counter Attacks

Listen to what your keeper is saying in counter attacks. A part of his responsibility here is to make his teammates aware of any unseen threats. This will include notifying you of any opponents overlapping or sneaking up from behind the defense line.

The goalie also warns you of any tricky play that you can't read. This might be a chip-through pass coming in over your head, for example.

Counter attacks are usually fast, chaotic and sensitive to quick decisions. Oftentimes, a goal is conceded from a counter attack as a result of the errors made by the defending team.

This is more likely than the attacking skills of the other team. So it means you have to listen out for anything your keeper tells you. In short, being in sync with the goalie means you can better respond to any threat coming at the goal.

OK, this is the communication of the goalkeeper. The second type of communication is the one you have with your other defensive teammates.

This should be about:

Any Change in the Attacking Formation of the Opposite Team

This is something that occurs a lot. Changes in the opponent's formation happen quickly in counter attacks, made by them against you. In these situations, many defenders are often busy monitoring the ball and tracking running opponents.

This means they are unaware of any uncovered attackers sneaking up to occupy an empty space. They then stand patiently by, often quite unnoticed, as they wait for the ball. These are smart moves that often result in victory when gone unchallenged.

In these situations it is important that the defensive players coordinate with each other. It is especially important for the two center backs.

They need to make a fast decision about who will to go out and meet the attacker and who should stay in position. One needs to stay put to mark any opportunistic opponent looking for an empty space or a better position.

If you watch a lot of soccer then you may have noticed an all too common mistake made by defenders. It is when two defenders go after the ball, thus leaving one opponent unmarked.

And we all know the advantages of being unmarked. It gives us a clear run and an opportunity to score or assist a goal.

Switching Positions

In a lot of cases, the leader of the two center backs (usually the captain) will switch roles with the other. He does this if he notices any signs of impatience or short temper when playing against a pushy attacker.

Distributing Roles

In free kicks and set pieces, defenders need to communicate with each other. They have to decide who marks who. This should be decided before the game begins, though things won't always go according to plan. Any change in the opposite team's tactics in free kicks and set pieces may require a change in your role inside the penalty area.

When Not Covering Their Position

Any right back (RB) or a left back (LB) with attacking tendencies can bring you lots of problems. This is especially so when they don't pay enough attention to covering the space they leave behind when attacking or assisting on the other side of the field.

This is something that is most likely to happen when they get tired and lose focus, like at the end of the second half.

When Calling for the Offside Trap

Please refer to the earlier section of this book where we covered the offside trap in considerable detail.

12. Not Adapting to Changes in the Playing Strategy

Anytime a player from your team gets sent off things can end up quite messy. Your coach will have to make changes in the team's playing strategy too. When this happens he starts by making a substitution. He will enter a defensive player if the man sent off was a back or a defensive midfielder "a stopper."

The gaps between all the three lines of your team (the attack, the midfield and the defense) need reducing as much as possible. This is most important for the space between the defenders and the midfielders.

When these changes happen and you're leading in the score, wait until the other team starts to look for a goal before changing your strategy. You then play long, accurate through passes to the front whenever is possible.

And whenever you have the chance, calm the play down. Do this by absorbing the other team's attacking energy with lots of passes.

If the other team is winning, their players will tend to use short passes between themselves. This is so that they can maintain ball control and possession since they're already anticipating attacks from your side.

In these situations, your team should never rush in with full on attacks. If you do this, you will leave behind spaces that the opposition can use for counter attacks. You should also pass the ball often, until you find a chance to score.

You will depend mostly on corners, headers, fouls and shooting from outside the penalty area. Only go for full on attacks in the last 10 minutes or so of the game. This is when the other team will be trying to play things safe, in their attempts to secure the score.

At this point, you or your fellow center back, or both of you, will have to switch roles with your defensive midfielders.

This is so that they can cover your backs when you move forward to help in corner kicks and crosses. Note that in general, enter backs are better at dealing with high balls, crosses and headers than midfielders.

If you are a right or left back, you will have to send a lot of crosses. Most of these will be just away from the penalty area.

This is because the other team will be compact back in defense. That means it will be harder for you, or your fellow winger, to run on the flank and penetrate, or even send close range crosses.

If you're a good shooter, try to go deeper inside the field and fire a strong ball every now and then. Even if it doesn't work out, after a shot or two, rival defenders will start to take notice of you.

They may then send a player to mark you whenever you try to go deeper. What this can do is help to free up your winger. It gives him an extra space to run into before the ball gets passed to him.

13. Not Providing Extra Coverage on the Goal Line

One of the top three soccer defenders today is the Borussia Dortmund's center back and the German world champion. His name is Mats Hummels.

Hummles recently declined an offer from Manchester United to become the most expensive center back in the game's history. He simply preferred to stay with his German side. He is, without any question of doubt, one of the best defenders, if not the best, to provide coverage on the goal line.

Any time he feels danger, he will read the attack. He then lets his teammates face the attackers or the player having the ball. Hummles will then retreat a little so that he can position himself on the goal line, or close to it. He usually positions himself in just the right place, ready to clear the ball away once it reaches him or passes his goalkeeper.

This act is like a habit. It is something that Hummles does even in free kicks. In many direct free kicks near the penalty area, and facing the goal (18 – 22 yards away from the goal), it's wise to ask the keeper if he needs any extra cover on the goal line.

Even if this move covers the offside trap, your keeper may still need someone to stand on the goal line with him. This might be right next to the far post.

Because Hummles is smart, he manages to combine good coverage without breaking the offside trap. Let's look at how he does this using a real example to illustrate. Anytime his team faces a foul on the edge of the penalty area, Hummles will stand in the free kick wall. Here is where he waits until the opponent starts to play the free kick. Once the play begins, then, and only then, Hummles will move over to the goal line.

Take a look on the internet for one great save that illustrates his skill. It was against TSG Hoffenheim 1899. Here Hummles retreated to the goal line and used his head to block a shot that was about to enter the net. With great skill he managed to direct the ball toward the corner.

Like all great players, Hummles makes his job look easy. It's not, of course, but he makes it look that way. You can learn a lot by studying the way these great players defend their goals.

14. Not Pressuring the Referee

Never be afraid to put pressure on the referee. I would say always put pressure on the ref when you need to. You can do this by asking for fouls and for protesting against any of his decisions that seem to favor the rival side. So question his decisions whenever a foul is in doubt.

Question his decisions whenever he makes a mistake. And always ask the referee to defend you if your opponent is getting a little too aggressive.

And when necessary, have your teammates surround the referee and talk to him as a group. This tactic is especially useful if you feel he's favoring the other side for whatever reason.

F.C. Barcelona and Atletico Madrid are two of the most successful soccer teams around today. They are also two of the most effective teams when it comes to dealing with referees.

Players of both sides are incredibly effective at pressuring refs. In fact, any game between the two sides becomes an out and out nightmare for any referee taking that game. Let's look at a couple of examples of how they do this.

Case 1: F.C Barcelona

F.C. Barcelona has a lot of talented players. This includes the likes of Messi, Neymar, Luis Suarez and Andres Iniesta. So much talent in one team puts a lot of pressure on any side that challenges them.

Other teams often feel that the only way to beat the superstars is by using excessive aggression. So they go in with too much hard tackling and barging.

Because of this threat, Barcelona players feel that they need protecting a lot more than most other teams.

This all began with the hugely successful Barcelona team of 2007. It was a time when they emerged with their Tiki-Taka playing style. Their high scoring rates bothered all other teams pitted against them. Frustrated rival players would start to get too aggressive.

In fact, this rough playing style set a precedent for anyone up against the Barcelona side. Ronaldinho and Messi in particular were having a tough time of it all.

As a result of this rough treatment, the Barca players realized that there was only one way to deal with this type of severe aggression. Their solution was to complain to the ref, and complain hard. So they would gather around him in a group.

From there they would pressure him to stop their opponents from using undue force against them. They would hound the ref with every single tackle made against any of them. They would even do it when the tackle wasn't aggressive.

As a result of this tactic they gained the protection they needed, but that's not all. Because they got good at forcing the ref to keep a watchful eye on their opponents, their own work on the field became even easier.

All referees know that Messi is an international treasure who needs safety and protection. Because of who he is, he's vulnerable to all kinds of aggressive behavior. Opponents know that refs are always looking out for soccer's Golden Boy.

This is good news for Messi but not such good news for his opponents. In many situations his rivals will not dare to go in too hard against him. They fear that making a hard tackle against this guy might get them booked or even sent off. In other words, Messi's challengers will often pussyfoot around him.

You can check the YouTube vids for yourself. You will find a plethora of clips with incidents for Barcelona players. Look out for the likes of Dani Alves and their defensive midfielder Sergio Busquets. These guys often deceive the referee with fake dives and fake injuries.

Many of these incidents result in fouls for their side and bookings against those playing against them. Since all referees are now programmed to protect Barcelona players, the team gets away with all sorts. This is a classic case of whatever brings results gets repeated.

Case 2: Atletico Madrid

The second team that has become adept at pressuring referees is Atletico Madrid. Their story started back in 2011. It was at a time when Diego Simeone took his new position as the head coach with the team he used to play for back in the 1990s.

Simeone, the former Argentine captain for more than eight years, is well-known for his high spirits. This is a man who has a strong winning mentality. Some people interpret his enthusiastic style as aggression. Whether you like him or not, this is a man who gets results.

The first thing Simeone did when he arrived at Madrid was to take everything he knew about winning and pour it all into the hearts and minds of his players.

It worked too. He managed to turn Atletico Madrid's players into real warriors; guys who would stop at nothing to win. Even if they had to play rough soccer to triumph, they would do whatever it took.

Of course, any kind of excess roughness in soccer can lead to getting booked a lot. And Atletico Madrid had now become a pretty rough side.

Because of this, Simeone and his assistants needed to protect themselves from referees, many of whom were on constant lookout for any misbehavior.

It was time for them to adopt a new tactic, and Simeone knew just what to do. So Atletico Madrid started to take the "Let's Pressure The Referee" approach. They thought it would be a good way to avoid getting red and yellow cards. So did it work?

Watch any of Atletico Madrid's games and you will see for yourself. You will note how the players gang up on the refs all the time. In fact, they protest after just about every serious decision made by a referee.

You can find them talking to him, shouting at him, and debating every decision he makes. They will also remind him of every single mistake he ever made during the game. It's fair to say that Atletico Madrid's players have become a ref's worst nightmare.

They can get a referee to the point where he may even give one of them a borderline foul. He may do this even if it's not really warranted.

Or he may avoid giving any of the team a yellow or red card. He does this just to save himself from grief and mind fatigue.

The Atletico Madrid players don't only pressure the ref either. They will happily bully the linesman as well, if need be.

So are these tactics fair? Well, soccer does have set rules, and everyone expects fair play and clean games in a perfect world.

But it's not a perfect world and soccer if a rough and tumble sport. That means teams and team players will often do whatever it takes to win.

If they find a winning formula, they won't worry too much whether it's the right thing to do or not. The only thing that matters is whether they get to produce results.

The higher up the leagues you go, the more pressure there is to triumph. So there's not always room for pleasantries or fair play in competitive soccer.

15. Not Able to Control Your Temper

As a defender, you should always try to keep calm and composed. This is even more important when there's a lot of stress going on in a game. One of the main stresses a defender faces is from the striker playing against him.

In some games you will face attackers who will try to wind you up big time. This is all part of their mental game.

They do it to intimidate you. If they are successful, and you get agitated, then your performance declines. When that happens, it's one nil to the striker. So just how do these intimidating tactics work?

Well, he will try to taunt you whenever you're within earshot. He will make jokes and perhaps even throw insults your way, mocking all your attempts to defeat him.

His goal is to distract you to the point where you lose focus. If he can get you riled by his taunting, so much the better.

And he's even more successful if he can get you to make an aggressive reaction. If the ref sees you lashing out in a fit of temper, he will give you a yellow or even a red card. If that happens, your team becomes outnumbered and it's a two nil win for the striker. As far as he's concerned, it's a job well done.

Losing your temper does not help you or your side. Some players are expert at taunting their opponents. They know just what buttons to push to get the reactions they want.

Your secret weapon here is to always expect someone to try this tactic. At least this way you can prepare yourself before the game. Knowing how you will respond, or not respond, before it happens is your best defense.

There are some exceptional defenders out there who will never make the big time. They have all the physical skills necessary, but physical talent alone is not enough. If you can't remain calm and composed when the pressure is on, then you can't expect to go far in soccer.

Or if you do make it, you won't be around for too long, not once your short temper is exposed. Some talented players are just too sensitive and easy to wind up.

Because of this, many never make it to the high levels of soccer. No big soccer club is ever going to knowingly invest in a player who can't keep his cool and control his temper. He will just be more trouble than he's worth.

There are other times when this approach backfires on the one doing the taunting. What happens is the player they are trying to upset actually feeds off their intimidation tactics. Yes, they get angry, but they don't show it in the way the one doing the taunting had hoped.

They channel their upset into their game. When they get to do this, they actually improve their defensive performance as a result. And the more the striker tries to wind them up, the better they play. Let's look at a real example to illustrate.

Joey Barton (bad boy Joe)

Let's look at Joey Barton as an example. He has heart, he is a real fighter on the field, and he has great defensive skills. There is, however, another side to Barton. Any attacker playing against him can unleash the angry child with the smallest of taunts. It doesn't take much at all to get Barton to show his aggressive side, and rival strikers know this.

Barton played for Newcastle United, and then won the English premier league with Manchester City. But after becoming a symbol of bad temper and aggressive behavior in English soccer, his career began to go south.

He went on to play for the below average team, Queens Park Rangers, which he relegated. He's now ending his career with Burnley F.C. in the second division.

Barton had fights with players from Arsenal, Manchester City, Liverpool and Blackburn Rovers. He once punched the Norwegian winger, Morten Gamst Pedersen, in the chest.

He gave Ryan Babel a bleeding nose. And he dropped his shorts to expose two peachy buttocks to the home fans of Norwich City after getting sent off. The list of bad incidents goes on and on.

Pepe (Képler Laveran Lima Ferreira)

Another example of aggressive behavior is the central defender Pepe. He is a Portuguese professional soccer player who plays for Spanish club Real Madrid and the Portuguese national team.

Pepe is one of the most - if not the most - aggressive, bad tempered defensive soccer players of the last 20 years. He's also one of the most skilled defenders in the world right now. That's the only reason he's still hanging on to his career.

Despite securing a place in Real Madrid's defense, Pepe's main disadvantage is that he loses his temper real easy. It doesn't take much to get him all hot and bothered.

Whether it's a verbal taunt from an opponent, or the game just isn't going his way, Pepe can explode at any moment. To say he has a short fuse is an understatement.

In one game in the Spanish league, the attacker playing against Pepe tried to fake a dive inside the goal area. This is something soccer players do at times in the hope of getting a penalty. Well, that act was enough to trigger Pepe's fiery temper.

He kicked that player in the legs, hard too, followed by a kick to his back as he went to the ground. Then, a few seconds later he went back to the player and kicked him again, this time grabbing him by the hair.

He then tried to start a fight with the player's teammates as they came to defend their buddy. Needless to say that Pepe got a red card for his unacceptable behavior.

He then went on to trash-talk the referee and the lines man. It was an ugly incident, that's for sure. Some would argue that Pepe is not just hot-tempered but completely unhinged.

As a result of the incident above, Pepe got a ban for eight months. This caused a lot of problems for his team. They couldn't replace him either, since the transfer market had already ended.

This incident was not a one-off. Pepe's aggressiveness kept showing up even after he returned from his long ban. He gave the French left back, Aly Cissokho, a martial arts kick in one game. This happened in the Champions league with Lyon Vs Real Madrid.

There's also Pepe's aggressive attitude against Barcelona players in general. It has become something of a disadvantage for Real Madrid. This is because whenever they play against each other, the referee has to be extra vigilant.

He has to protect Barcelona players against Pepe's violent outbursts. This tension sometimes results in unfair, mistaken decisions.

Heck, refs have enough to do managing a game as it is. Having to babysit players with temper tantrums is the last thing they need.

Costa Vs. Paulista

Here's a case from the North London Derby between Chelsea and Arsenal. During the game, Chelsea's striker, Diego Costa, hit Arsenal`s defender, Laurent Koscielny, three times.

Costa is well-known for being sneaky, pushy and playing against the rules. Because of that, his misconduct is no big surprise. Neither the referee nor the linesman saw this actual incident though, but what happened next was interesting.

Koscielny's partner, Gabriel Paulista, saw what had happened to his teammate. He then went over to Costa and picked a fight with him.

The ref saw this and had no choice but to give both of them a yellow card. Just 20 seconds later, Costa then went over to Paulista and began cursing him. He then hit Paulista from behind when the ref wasn't looking, and waited for him to respond.

His plan was to throw himself to the ground the moment the ref turned to look in their direction. If his plan worked, the referee would have no choice but to send the Arsenal defender off for bad behavior.

So did it work? Yes, it did, it worked like a charm. Gabriel Paulista got sent off and Costa continued to play and help lead his team to a 2- 0 win against their rivals.

The moral of the above account is twofold. The first is to avoid being a hero and stay out of fights that don't directly involve you.

At least while the game is on. And the second is to know how to control your temper. Paulista wasn't the one who got whacked at the beginning.

He could have just notified the referee of the incident. Instead, he decided to play the superhero and sort things out himself. His actions might at first seem like a gallant act, but it was actually a stupid decision. Because of his misconduct, his team then had to play the rest of the game with 10 players instead of 11.

There will be times when you play against an attacker who tries to mess with your mind.

The important thing here is to understand what he's doing and why he's doing it. When he curses you, or physically attacks you, you must avoid reacting with reciprocal force.

This is exactly what he wants you to do, so don't play his little game by taking the bait. Instead, keep calm and try to ignore him. The best way to get your revenge is to play well and prevent him from reaching the ball.

The Zinedine Zidane Fiasco

Look at the incident between Zinedine Zidane and Marco Materazzi in the 2006 World Cup final game. France's Zinedine Zidane was playing his last-ever game when he got sent off. What he did was head-butt Italy's Marco Materazzi's hard in the chest.

It was in retaliation to Materazzi trash-talking him. I don't condone the act by any means, but Materazzi was successful at pressuring Zidane. He got him so riled that he just snapped.

The attacking midfielder was then out of the game. This is exactly what Materazzi had hoped would happen. How upset had he made Zidane with his trash-talking?

Well, let's just say that Zidane said he would rather die than apologize to Marco Materazzi. That's a pretty successful taunt on Materazzi's part.

If Zidane had kept calm and remained focused on the game, the outcome might have been quite different. He could have actually helped France win their second World Cup title.

But he didn't. He will probably spend the rest of his life blaming himself for destroying their chances. If you ever get angry, channel that anger into your game, not your temper.

There will always be some players who try to destroy your focus. It is part of who they are. It is in fact, one of their mental game strategies.

They will mess with you first in a psychological sense, usually by trash-talking and mocking. If that fails, they may then try the physical approach and push or whack you. In other words, they will do whatever it takes to prevent you from keeping your head in the game.

The more of a threat you are to them, the harder they will try to mess with your focus or get you sent off the field. These players are aggressive because they fear you. And because of this they want you out of the way.

Always remember that this is usually just a tactic, it's not personal, even though it might seem personal at the time.

When you take the bait and lash out, it is one nil to the attacker. If you ignore them and play even better, it's an own goal for them. Which would you prefer?

16. You Face the Attacker with Your Side

If you take the role of the right or left back, you will encounter lots of one-to-one situations. These will typically be between you, and the winger playing against you. This also applies to center backs facing opponents in counter attacks.

In these situations, make sure your body faces the guy with the ball head-on as much as possible.

Oftentimes, a defender will approach the attacker from his side. He does this thinking he has a better chance at intercepting any pass the attacker plays.

This sounds good in theory, but it's not so good in practice. The reason is simple. Most attackers prefer to feint or dribble in one-to-one situations, not pass the ball.

I think an attacker would get pass you with the ball more than 80 percent of the time if you come at him from the side.

In some cases you have to show him your side so that you can prepare to run after him if picks up the pace.

But he will more than likely beat you when he shoots off anyway. So your best option is to always try and get the ball before he starts to run.

17. Not Perfecting Your Decision Making Process

As a defensive player, you will often face situations where you have to choose between several decisions. This is also something you will have to do fast. You can have the build of a solid defender, but on its own build is no use.

Without the right mindset and decision-making skills, you won't ever make it as a professional. This is especially the case if you're playing in the back line.

OK, let's look at how you can develop your decision-making ability.

There is a simple process you can follow that will help in this area. It consists of three basic stages. These stages are: the bulking stage, the filtering stage and the blocking stage. The last one is the "not thinking" stage. OK, we will now go through each of these stages in turn.

The Bulking Stage

The only thing this stage requires is that you become aware of what you do and how you think. In other words, you need to start taking notes of what's going on inside the playing ground. It is, to all intents and purposes, a fact finding mission.

We all make mistakes, but we don't always take too much notice of them at the time. A defender will usually just move on with the game and think no more about his slip. Well, that all has to stop. It is only when you can identify flaws in your game that you get to work on them.

There can be no solutions until you first know what the problem areas are. So in this stage you will need to take a lot of notes over time. Don't just write down the areas you fall short on either. Make notes also on what you do right.

What you are doing here is building a complete picture of your game. The more mistakes you identify, the more you get to work on your game. To build a complete profile you need to play in lots of different situations. Start off by playing different types of passes.

Keep the attacker in front of you in one situation, and then try to stay behind him in another. Switch roles with different defenders and play against different types of attackers. These will typically be the fast, the strong, the talented, the pushy, and so on.

The most important thing is to try and play in as many different situations as possible. You need to expose yourself to lots of new things.

Remember to write it all down. You will be amazed at what you discover about yourself and your style of play.

Some of it will be impressive; other areas will need work. Whenever you get home from training or a game, take a little time out to write down everything you can recall. Remember to include good play as well as bad. The more get down on paper, the more effective this stage will be.

The Filtering Stage

The filtering stage is where you gather all the data you have written down about your game. It's now time to turn all those notes into a single manual. Separate the good play from the bad.

If you have been precise in your note taking, it should all make sense when you start to reread stuff. It will include notes like: When "X" happened I should have done "Y," and when dealing with "A" it would have been better to do "C" rather than "B."

You job here is to filter all your data, separating it so that you get a complete profile. Once you have a few weeks or months of data, you will start to notice certain patterns in your game.

I can promise you this: by getting your game down on paper, you will learn more about yourself and the way you perform than talking about it ever could.

The Not Thinking Stage

This is the stage where you don't think you just do. It is where you start working from your manual. You are no longer writing stuff down and analyzing it.

You have already done that in the first two stages. By now you should have identified any flaws in your game and have the solutions in place to fix them.

You can fix some areas of you game just by changing your approach. Other areas will need you to work more on improving an existing skill, or learning something new.

The point is that you now know what you're good at. You also know what needs work, and what, if anything, needs removing altogether.

Many years ago, when I first worked on these stages, I found out a lot about the way I played. I saw that I often wasted a few moments by following the path of at a crossed ball through the air, as one example. I fixed this by running toward the ball every time, so that I could reach it before the player I was marking.

That tiny shift in the way I responded to these balls made a big difference to my game. I also noticed how I would often forget about the guy I was marking and stray away.

Again, my game improved when I started to give full focus to my designated role. These things and more besides changed my mindset, my attitude, and my style of play for the better.

Sometimes in soccer, tweaking small things can make the biggest difference. This is a fast paced game that needs quick thinking followed by fast actions.

When you work through the three stages outlined in this chapter, and then take positive actions, great things will come to pass.

18. Not Feeling Ok with Sending the Ball to the Outside

Another mistake that many defenders make is an all too common one. It is when they fail to err on the side of safety and try to run the show, irrespective of the consequences.

Hogging the ball is never a good idea when you're under attack. It is a particular problem among amateurs and young defenders who don't have enough experience to play a more mature game.

They often try to use their own skills instead of passing the ball to their nearest teammate. They also refuse to send a long ball toward the opposite side of the field, or send it to a throw outside the field. They are not ok with playing safe; they're too excited about having the ball.

A good player is well-rounded. He knows when to run with things and when to pass the game on to others.

In modern soccer, you should be able to take on different roles on the field. One of these roles is to play as a stopper or a defensive midfielder. Before you can do this well, you first have to let go of being the star of the show.

The role of a stopper requires a tough player who's a decision maker. He has a great ability for defusing and shutting down the rival team's attacks. He does this before the ball even reaches his defensive line.

To be able to play as a stopper you have to be ok with sending the ball to the outside. You also have to be ok with not holding onto the ball and starting an attack of your own. For the stopper, playing safe always comes before attacking.

Super Mascherano

In the 2014/2015 season, Barcelona won four major trophies. These were the Spanish league, the Champions league, the UEFA Super cup and the Copa Del Rey cup.

You can attribute a lot of these victories to the performance of their offensive trio, namely, Leo Messi, Neymar Jr., and Luis Suarez. But this was not a three man show. Barcelona's great success is also thanks to having Javier Mascherano as their defensive midfielder.

Mascherano is a soccer icon. He helped lead Argentina to the final of the World Cup in 2014 and in the final of Copa America in 2015. He was the only player in Barcelona's defensive line that could play well in all the defensive positions.

His main role is defensive midfielder, but he adapts well to other roles too, and performs with impressive skill. Anytime a player from the back line got injured, Mascherano would step up to the plate and fill the gap.

Mascherano plays his defensive midfielder role by the book. He rarely plays with style or seeks his own glory. For him, it's always the team that comes first. So when it comes to defusing an attack he focuses only on destroying the opponent's passes, doing whatever it takes.

If he has to send the ball to the outside, then he does it. Mascherano formula is classic and focused. He takes the right position, plays with aggression, and keeps the ball away. That's it, in a nutshell. Simple in theory, a lot harder in practice, but he does a fantastic job more often than not.

If you ever watch Mascherano play, you can see the simplicity in his style. He positions himself in the center, between the ball the player receiving it. Or he might take a ready–to–run position behind the player who's waiting to receive the ball.

He does this so that he can outrun that player to that ball once it leaves the passer's foot. Once he reaches the ball, he clears it away without too much lag. It's classic defending.

Anytime Mascherano feels in trouble, or is unable to direct the ball to a teammate, he sends it to the outside. He does this without a moment's hesitation. Either that or he kicks the ball as hard as he can toward the other team's side.

His main concerns, which should be yours too, is to kill the attack before thinking about starting a new one. Killing the attack to him is definitely more important than trying to look good.

Javier Mascherano is the beast behind Barcelona's beautiful game. No one will dispute that he gives the team balance, both on and off the field.

19. Unable to Play in Different Defensive Roles

In modern soccer, being adaptable accounts for a lot. The more flexible and adaptable a player is to different game plans, the higher his price tag. That means the bigger, better clubs are more likely to snap him up. Today, all the big coaches look for players who can take on different roles on the field.

Not only do they expect them to play in different positions, but they expect them excel too. This applies to all positions, not only defenders. The expectations of coaching greats like Pep Guardiola, Jose Mourinho and Carlo Ancelotti are set high these days.

They will even look for goalkeepers who can adapt to their different game plans when need be. Just look at what Manuel Neuer does for the German national team, as well as his own team Bayern Munich. They call him "The Sweeper Keeper".

Neuer's price tag is at least 20 million dollars above other professional goalkeepers. Besides being fantastic at keeping his goal safe, Neuer also knows how to play crosses and create effective counter attacks. He can also play as a sweeper or Libero.

As a sweeper, he predicts and intercepts the majority of through passes and long balls played behind his defensive line.

Watch his game with Germany against Algeria in the last Brazilian World Cup. You will quickly see why he is so valuable. He gives his team the opportunity to attack by one extra player.

In their game against Chelsea, in the UEFA Super Cup, Neuer made an assist to one of his teammates from Chelsea's own half. That's something a defender or a midfielder should do. It's not what you would usually expect from a goalkeeper. This is why so many clubs are willing to pay more than seventy or eighty million Euros to buy a keeper like Neuer.

Sergio Ramos – The 10th Champions League

In the 2014 UEFA Champions league, Real Madrid had a major problem on their hands before the final game.

It was when their main and most talented defensive midfielder, Xavi Alonso, was prevented from playing. What happened was that Alonso had reached his limit of yellow cards in the semifinal.

The meant that Real Madrid's coach at that time, Carlo Ancelotti, had a dilemma on his hands. He had to either choose between using one of Alonso's substitutes or find his team a different, extraordinary solution.

What did he do? Well he didn't give the defensive midfielder's role to one of the team's other midfielders. Instead, Ancelotti chose to put his defensive player, Sergio Ramos, in the stopper role.

This turned out to be the perfect decision. Ramos stepped up to the challenge and played one of the best games of his life. Thanks to his ability to adapt, Madrid went on to win their 10th Champions League title.

Ramos even went out and scored a last minute equalizer in the 94th minute. The game went into extra time where Ramos' teammates scored three more goals. This ended in a 4–1 triumph to Real Madrid over their neighbors Atletico Madrid.

David Alaba

Another example of an over qualified defensive player is the Austrian international, David Alaba. At the time of writing, Alaba plays for Bayern Munich.

Besides being one of the best free kick takers in Europe, and indeed the world, Alaba can take on any role on the defensive line. He can play just as well as a center back as a defensive midfielder. He can even play well on both sides, as a left or right back.

This is because he has learned to use both of his feet with equal efficiency. He can send crosses using any foot with great power and world class precision.

These are the reasons why his Bayern Munich coach, Pep Guardiola, love him so much. David Alaba can slot into any position and in any game plan that the Spanish coach uses.

Last year the club was asked if they would sell Alaba. One of FC Bayern's executives, I guess it was Karl-Heinz Rummenigge, let his thoughts known about that. He said they would rather sell their entire coaching staff and executive team before even considering selling Alaba. And to think he's only 23 years old.

As you can see, the more you can do, the more indispensable you become. If you want to turn into a well-rounded, complete player, you can do that if you have the right commitment.

But it won't come easy. It means you will have to eat, sleep and breathe soccer. You will have an unrelenting desire to become complete.

You will have to find every single one of your weak points and work at sharpening them all. Even if you have natural talent, that won't do you any good on its own. You still need to have patience, persistence, and a relentless desire to reach the top of your game.

The second thing you should do is examine every area of your game. Get others to give you constructive feedback as well. Prepare to hear stuff you would sooner not hear.

Sometimes, others can see in us what we fail to see in ourselves. It's not nice to hear others point out our faults, but you still have to invite constructive feedback all the same.

It's certainly necessary if you're serious about becoming great. So take an honest look at every aspect of your game and see what you need to work on. Any areas where you're bad or average are the areas you need to zoom in on first and improve without delay.

Look at what You Are Good At

You also need to look at what you're good at and see if there is anything to can take further from those areas.

If you're good at reading tactics and plays, for example, then why not do what Pep Guardiola did while he was playing at Barcelona. That is to put time and effort into studying your opponent as well as other team's tactics and game styles.

Guardiola began his career as a slightly above average defensive player. He had quite a weak body and average shooting skills.

By improving his major skills he became a master at reading the game. He got so good at this that he became able to read passes and plays before they even happened.

Aside from developing his game-reading skills, Guardiola also improved in other areas as well. He worked hard at developing his physical and mental abilities. As a result of his efforts, Guardiola was able to become one of the most talented stoppers to ever play for Barcelona.

Once you identify the areas where you need to improve, you have to also ask yourself what it is you lack. By that I mean maybe there's a way to do something that you have never tried before. In other words, apart from developing existing skills, you may also need to learn new ones from scratch.

It all depends what your goals are. Without an objective, you won't go anywhere far. So before you even start on your journey to greatness, start by asking yourself these two questions:

"Using my current skills, what else can I offer my team? And how can I increase my assisting and my goal-scoring ratio?"

Another Step Further: Play with Both Legs Equally

Look for any skill, or a tendency, or an attacking desire that you own. Once you have it, get to work on improving it every single day.

You may have a strong foot or have good shooting skills that need enhancing still further. Keep your focus set on becoming great at fouls or at shooting from outside the penalty area.

You may need to enhance your headers, which is something you must be good at anyway. No matter how good you are at something, see what you can do to become even better. Perhaps you can work at improving your passing skills if you need to.

This way you will be in a better position to create decent counter attacks or in-depth passes. This will help you penetrate through the opponent's defensive line and create serious danger.

Finally, try playing in all the defensive positions for a reasonable amount of time. You're young and that means you have time on your side. So every once in a while try to switch positions with any of your teammates.

Ask your coach to test you in different roles, even if they are offensive ones. The more you try, the better you will get to know what works for you. Then, and only then, will you discover what you need to do to take your game up to a whole new level.

Can you play with your left and right foot with equal accuracy and strength? If not, then you need to start learning.

This is one of the most important things that a complete defensive player must be able to do. Playing with both legs has so many advantages.

First, it enables you to play on both flanks, as a right or a left back. Second, it helps you pass the ball anywhere on the field.

By doing this you get to create more spaces and dangerous counter attacks. Third, being able to use both legs to shoot the ball is crucial to any defensive midfielder.

This is because you will sometimes find yourself receiving balls on the edge of the penalty area. If you're good enough, you'll be able to smash these balls toward the net without a moment's hesitation.

If you're not good enough, you will waste valuable time trying to get the ball under control using your dominant foot. Finally, you should know how to send direct, fast and accurate crosses using both of your feet.

The best of the best on the flanks are the wingers and the full backs that are able to send a cross while running. They don't need to stop and waste time trying to switch feet before playing the cross.

And anyway, the curvy crosses, the ones played with the same foot of the same side, are more effective. They create more danger for the opponent's goal than the ones played with opposite feet.

Let's assume your dominant foot is your left one. And let's say you are forced to play on the right side, as a RB. In this situation, most of your crosses will be useless.

Even if they are kind of "OK," they will still be easy for the rival defenders to clear away. That's unless you know how to play crosses with your right foot of course.

I know that you can be good or even great with one foot. Many great players are indeed one-footed. But still, you don't have the luxury of choosing where and how you should receive the ball. How you get to play depends on your ability to use both your legs equally.

Look at the most successful and the most valuable strikers in football right now. You will find that almost all of them can play with both feet equally, and with impressive accuracy too.

Most amateur players don't bother developing their weaker foot. They think it's too awkward, impossible even. But it's not. All you have to do is push past that awkwardness.

Even if it seems impossible, comical even, don't give up. I can promise you that as long as you stick with it, you will be able to use your weaker foot before too long. Best of all is that you will get to use it with more power and accuracy than you can possibly imagine.

OK, let's look at how you can make a start at improving your weaker foot.

Begin with the Basics

First you have to start slow. This is just until your weaker foot gets used to the ball. So the way to introduce your weak foot to the game is to begin with some easy drills. This will include things like passing the ball with the weak foot.

You can also kick it against a wall and then receive it with the same foot. Once you get comfortable with these things, start to flip the ball and do some back heel kicks. With these drills you get to use both the inside and the outside of your weakest foot.

Focus on Accuracy

You will need some foul sticks for this first accuracy drill. Put them in various locations on the field. Once in place, aim at the foul sticks from different angles and positions using your weakest foot.

Your goal here is to focus on accuracy and the sensitivity of your leg. Don't worry if the balls come out weak or look inferior to those you send with your dominant foot.

In fact, you should expect a lesser performance at this early stage. Just do you best for now, knowing that with each practice progress is inevitable.

Run and Play on the Side

Place one foul stick in the middle of the penalty area or a bit closer to the goal. Now run on the side, the side of your weak foot, and start playing crosses toward that stick.

What you should do here is keep your cross as curvy as possible. Try to also make it hit the stick or at least make the ball go a few centimeters above the stick.

By doing this you can simulate the situation of sending a cross to a teammate, who will usually have to jump to reach the ball.

Work on Your Power

Take different positions outside the penalty area (both near and far). Work on sending fast, strong balls toward the upper and lower corners of the goal. This is the toughest part, but you will have to keep working at it to perfect your shots.

Try to play them as if you're in a real game. In other words, see if you can fake a little real-world pressure into the situation. Imagine there are spectators watching you as you practice.

This stage may take you a few weeks of continuous practice before you get comfortable and good. Whatever you do, don't give in to frustration if the task seems futile. Just keep at it. I can promise you that progress will come.

What will probably happen is that you just start practicing one day and it all clicks into place. That's often the experience of many. Once you get good at this drill, you can then work on playing backwards and bicycle kicks using the now 'not so weak' foot.

Revisit all the drills above until you feel comfortable using your weaker foot. That means the basics, accuracy, playing on the side, and power.

Once you do get used to using this foot, you will never have to go through these initial feelings of awkwardness ever again.

Not only will it feel great knowing you can now use both your legs, but it's going to move your game up to a whole new level too.

20. You Don`t Position Yourself Well

Former Dutch professional player and manager, Johan Cruyff, has a special way of looking at soccer. He also has a distinctive way of talking about the game. Here's a quote of his about what defines a great player:

"When you play a match, it is statistically proven that players actually have the ball three minutes on average ... so, the most important thing is: what do you do during those 87 minutes when you do not have the ball. That is what determines whether you're a good player or not."

As a player and a defender, it's how you position yourself on the field that's important. It is something that can either make you or break you. A defender's success is how well he intercepts the ball (the pass). This will depend on three things.

1. Pick the best place to intercept the ball before it reaches the opponent next to you.

Always ask yourself where the next pass will be heading to. Once you know, or suspect you know, put yourself in a position that will allow you to intercept the pass.

If the pass is coming to the man you're marking, stay behind him. This lets you come up and steal the ball just before it reaches him.

If you think the passer will send a diagonal ball toward his teammate, move nearer to that teammate. This will allow you to slide and grab the ball before it reaches him.

2. Stand low to the ground.

Like the start of a 100 meter race, you will need to be in the "ready set go" position. I'm talking about the standup position here, not the one where your hands touch the floor.

Your ready position starts with the head tilt. It might not sound like much, but the way you position your head determines how well you get to sprint off and run for the ball.

When you tilt your head correctly, it straightens your neck and back. This brings your neck and back into the right alignment for a fast take off. It's important to let your gaze guide you.

That means you have to look ahead, not down at your feet. Keep a strong focus on the play as you prepare for the off. Your torso needs to be leaning forward a bit with your weight on the front part of your feet, just before the toes.

Although you might feel that the ready-set-go position comes natural, it's always a good idea to ask your coach if you've got it right. Sometimes, a minor tweak can make a big difference.

The start position in brief: Feet about shoulder width apart. Around 2/3rds of the weight is on the front foot. Bend the knees and lean slightly forward. Arms synchronized with the legs. Back, neck and head in line. That's it.

3. Position yourself behind the attacker.

In man-to-man marking, and when you're watching for an attacker, always position yourself behind him. You can either stick to him or keep a distance. What you can't do is have an attacker behind you when you receive the ball.

The reason is simple, in that you can't mark a player that you can't see. It's also the only way to prevent your opponent from turning and facing the goal. Anytime he turns, you'll be ready to block his shot by an interception or by a quick slide.

By taking the best position, you do make your life much easier. Any attempt from you to block a ball or intercept it won't come to much if you don't position yourself in the right place.

Once you're in the right position you can then choose between any of these three tackles; block, poke, and slide.

These are the common soccer tackling methods used to stop your opponents from scoring. We will now look at each of them in turn. Study them carefully and make sure you practice them well.

The Block Tackle

-   Close the distance and assume a defensive stance.
-   Draw your blocking foot and position it sideways.
-   Face your opponent, keeping your shoulders squared.
-   Move momentum forward and drive the blocking foot through the ball.
-   Keep your foot firm as you push the ball forward pass your opponent.
-   When you gain possession, try to begin an immediate counterattack.

The Poke Tackle

-   Start by closing the distance and assume the defensive stance.
-   Extend your tackling foot.
-   Flex your balanced leg.
-   Poke the ball with your toes.

- Withdraw your leg to avoid contact with your opponent.
- Chase and regain possession of the ball.

The Slide Tackle

- Approach from the side. Make the slide on your side and have your arms extended out to the sides for balance.
- Extend your lower leg and have your upper leg flexed at the knee.
- Use the instep of your lower leg to clear the ball away (try to avoid your opponent).
- Jump to your feet and collect the ball whenever possible.

Before you go in for the tackle you need to ask yourself the following questions. Don't worry about how many there are. This will all come natural to you, and in nanoseconds, once you are aware of your options.

- What are the potential shooting/passing angles available to me?
- How can I contain the ball holder and cover as many angles as possible?
- What are all the passing options available to the ball holder?
- How should I position myself so that I'm able to catch the next pass or cross before it reaches the man I'm marking?

- How to balance between keeping an eye on the man I'm marking and covering for my next teammate?
- When should I stick to my position and when should I leave it?
- What do I want from this situation and how can I force the ball holder to follow my plan of action?
- When should I interfere and how?
- Where am I from the penalty area? Where am I from the goal area/goal line? And where am I from my teammates (especially the nearest of them)?
- What's the next possible scenario for the ball holder to follow?
- What should I do if he gets past me?
- Which is my opponent's dominant foot (the one he uses most)? Which is my opponent's weakest foot (the one he uses least)? How can I best position myself so that I force him to use his weak foot?

They say that soccer only has two types of player, the goalkeeper and everyone else. But whatever your role is, each player needs to have different skills.

And because he has different roles he takes on different positions at various times. When you know how to position yourself well, you then get to make a huge difference to the way you perform.

21. You Continuously Get Dragged Outside the Penalty Area

One tactic that almost every team uses occurs when an attacker leaves the penalty area. What this does is drag the defender marking him outside the box.

Doing this clears an empty space for another attacker from the same team to come in and fill.

Pep Guardiola of Barcelona developed this tactic further. He decided to make Lionel Messi switch positions in and outside the penalty box. In effect, this changes him from being a winger to a false striker.

So he stays outside the penalty area until the moment is right. He then suddenly switches positions with Barcelona's main striker.

As he leaves the penalty area, he then creates a new space for Messi to come in and work his magic. They call this playing tactic the "false number 9." It has changed Messi's career from a talented winger to one of the best ever players in modern soccer.

Whenever you play against a team who has a lot of talented and creative midfielders, the pressure is always high.

There's also a lot of pressure playing against a team whose game plan relies on excessive passing. This includes sides like Barcelona, Arsenal and FC Bayern.

In these situations, you feel tempted to leave the penalty area, or from whatever position you're taking at the time.

It feels right and necessary to go after the player you're marking. My advice is not to do it.

You may recall in an earlier chapter where I said how you must mark the attacker you're responsible for at all times.

However, there is an exception to this. You can't apply the same rule outside the edge of the penalty area, especially if you are a center back.

You can always come and go with the knowledge that you've got cover when you play as a right or a left back. But you can't guarantee this when you're playing the center back role.

To be safe you must stick to your penalty area whenever the attacker you're marking goes outside it. Many attackers tend to draw back to the middle so that they can receive the ball from a better position.

When this happens, it's the role of the stopper and the rest of the midfielders to put pressure on him, not you.

As long as you are always mindful of this you will be in a better position to defend your team.

22. Not Being Effective on the Offensive Side

During the 20 or so years he has been playing for Chelsea FC, John Terry has scored a total of 39 goals.

This makes him the top scoring defender in the history of the English premier league. In fact, the brilliance of the goals he's scored doesn't just lie in their quality or timing.

The best thing about Terry's goals is that none of them came about from penalty kicks. This is the one thing that sets him apart from other famous goal scoring defenders, like Everton's legend Leighton Baines, as one example. We will look at Leighton Baines later.

Can you imagine how valuable a defender is who scores 39 goals for his team? He's a rare asset, that's for sure.

Of course, a professional, world class defender has to keep his goal safe, but that's not all he has to do. He must carry out offensive duties as well. As I mentioned earlier, coaches these days look for "complete players."

These are the guys who can not only perform their own roles to consistent high standards. They are also able to fill many other shoes outside their main role.

All Defenders: Chelsea Vs. PSG

If you watch football often you will know that more than 80 percent of a team's power lies in a strong, skilled back line. This is certainly the case when it comes to Chelsea. And it's most notable now that the Portuguese manger, Jose Mourinho, is in charge.

It's no coincidence that Chelsea's defensive line has three of the top 15 scoring defenders in Europe. This includes Terry, who's at top of that list.

There is one goal in particular that I would like you to study. It is in a game where Chelsea Vs Paris Saint Germain in the round of 16 game in the UEFA Champions league.

The game was in France and the French team was playing hard with full attacking power. Chelsea was now playing on the counter attack.

The game was moving in favor of the French when things all changed in the blink of an eye. Everyone, both on and off the field, wakes up as an exciting moment materializes.

Defender John Terry plays a cross to Gary Cahill (another defender). Cahill then assists the ball with a beautiful back heel kick toward Branislav Ivanovic (a third defender).

Ivanovic then scores with a wonderful header. Just for the record, Ivanovic has scored 22 goals for Chelsea in the past six years, at the time of writing.

To be a great defender, that's one who gets to score at times, there are a few essential skills you need to learn:

- Good shooting skills.
- Good passing skills (long passes and crosses).
- Good headers.
- Good penalties (when needed).

We will look at all these skills in more detail in the next four chapters, starting with the shooting skill.

23. Not Having Good Shooting Skills

You may have heard of a retired Brazilian player named Roberto Carlos. If not, don't worry. His name is not so important right now, it's his soccer legacy that we want to look at here.

Carlos, a World Cup winner, is perhaps the best left back to have played soccer in the last 25 years. In fact, he set a new standard for how a left and right back should play their game.

Before Carlos, the whole purpose of having a left or right back on the field was to stay tight and wait for the attack.

This was especially the case when the Catenaccio Italiano tactical system was in place. Catenaccio Italiano means "the Italian chain" in English. It was most famous in the 1980s and 90s as a tactical system with a strong emphasis on defense.

It was a strategy commonly used to better organize a team's defensive line. The idea was to defuse attacks from the opposition and play on the counter attacks or set pieces. But Carlos wasn't just a good solid left-back; he was the attacking solution every team dreamed of.

Carlos was fast. In fact, he was the fastest player in the world for an entire decade. He was so good with crosses that he managed to score goals from corner kicks and other dead spots close to the corner. The most important skill that Carlos had was his lethal left foot.

Despite his role as a left back, Roberto Carlos was second only to midfielder, Juninho Pernambucano, when it came to scoring goals from free kicks.

This was especially the case with free kicks played from far away. Typically, Carlos would pace 15-20 feet behind the ball, take a quick run, and then smash a super strong ball toward the opponent's goal.

Standing in the wall against Roberto Carlos was a nightmare for every defensive player. Some of his goals came about because the players standing in the free kick wall worried about their safety. It's true. They would move or dodge one of his balls rather than try to prevent it from reaching the goal. You have to see it to believe it. They would step away from the ball to avoid a whack from Carlos' flying missiles.

Roberto Carlos was so good at scoring from fouls. In actual fact, the best free kick ever scored was by him. It was against France in an exhibition game.

The free kick was 30 yards away from France's goal. Carlos moved back to the edge of the circle of the center line. He then took a long run and miraculously swung the ball with his left leg at a speed of 105 mph.

France's goalkeeper, Fabien Barthez, had no chance of saving it. All he could do was stand by and watch as the ball smashed into his net. You should be able to find the clip on YouTube. Just search for: Best free kick ever by Roberto Carlos 1997.

Strong accurate shooting is a really important skill for any defender. It is something you must become exceptional at. You need to strive to be as good as a real striker.

The way to do this is by improving in two areas. The first is your shooting accuracy and the second is your shooting power. Let's look at each of these in turn.

Shooting Accuracy

You rarely see a high profile player send a shot more than 10 or 20 inches outside the target area. A big miss happens from time to time, but it's far less likely than in amateur games, of course.

Skilled shooters have a good sense of where the goal is in relation to where they are. And so they know how and where they have to send the ball.

Their ability to follow-through with the shot is what makes their accuracy so good. Good accuracy and follow-through technique is something you will see in skilled players of all ball sports, not only soccer.

Do a quick search on YouTube for David Beckham and Roger Federer. You will see how these guys work miracles using their shooting skills. One uses his foot, the other his hand. Both are impressive.

It's a must that you practice to enhance your shots on a regular basis. This is not something you can do once and then forget about it.

Even when you can master powerful, accurate shots, you still have to maintain what you have. And the only way you can do that is to practice often. Remember to practice sending your balls from every position on the field too.

Pick unusual places on the field to train. Find the toughest angles and positions. Practice shooting from them over and over until you become great. Low balls, high balls, direct kicks, free kicks and more besides.

Don't leave a place untapped from where you can score a goal. When you practice like this, the less difficult places and positions around the field will become so much easier.

You need to create solutions for both yourself and your team whenever you feel stuck. So whenever you see a shooting opportunity or an extra space, take it.

Never shy away from something just because it seems difficult. It is only by pushing yourself and testing your limits that you get to grow.

I was watching a game once between Barcelona and A.S. Roma in the Champions league. The game was proving hard for the Italians, who were having a tough time reaching Barcelona's penalty area.

Despite playing in Rome, they were not faring well at all. Then, and to the surprise of many, the Italian side managed to score against Barca.

The goal came about when the Italian right Back, Alessandro Florenzi, sent a strong ball from a few meters above the center line (45-50 yards). The ball went over the keeper's head as it landed neatly in the goal.

This is the kind of thing you have to be able to do if you're to become a valuable defender. You must add value to your team whenever they need it. This is why you have to practice, and practice a lot.

No matter what advice you get on how to shoot a ball or how to increase your accuracy, knowledge alone is futile.

You won't see any improvement in your shooting style unless you act. Knowing how to do something is one thing. Actually doing it, is something else.

Don't ever get put off or frustrated when things don't go too well. Occasional setbacks are quite normal when trying to improve any skill.

The guys who become great are those who push forward no matter what setbacks come their way. You will learn the right shooting techniques not by your successful attempts, but by your failures.

It's true, we learn so much more from failure than we could ever hope to from success. So look at failed attempts as your friend. Learn from them, don't curse them, or beat yourself up. This is important.

Your shooting accuracy is proportional to the number of shots you practice at each training session. When you practice a lot of shots, your style will begin to develop naturally.

The 300 x 30 Routine

Here is an exercise you will want to perform daily. Do it either in the morning or before bedtime. Your task is to practice shooting 300 to 500 shots at the goal from different angles and places on the field.

Do this for 30 consecutive days. Don't skip a day or take a Sunday off either. Continuity is the key here. After 30 days you will marvel at just how much your performance has improved in a single month.

Here are five steps to follow to make your shots more powerful.

- Tighten your core (abs). This is so that you can make sure you're transmitting enough power from your body to the ball. It's like collecting energy before an explosion.
- Make sure you have free movement with your foot (the one that is to strike the ball). Again, this is so that you have enough energy to kick the ball hard.
- Do explosive one leg lunges:

How to Perform One-leg Lunges

Take the one leg lunges position. This means one leg is forward with the knee bent and the foot flat on the ground.

The other leg is behind. OK, when you come up, start kicking with your knee as if you're actually trying to strike someone with it.

This exercise will increase the explosiveness from your knees. It will help you to launch a fast kick with plenty of power. This is useful when a fast approaching opponent is putting pressure on you.

Run before you kick the ball – whenever possible

This will depend on where you receive the ball. It will also depend on the number of players around at the time of shooting. But whenever you can, try to run a little before striking the ball. This will provide you with the power necessary to reach your targets.

Learn from the masters

I encourage you to search video footage for both Zlatan Ibrahimovich and Hulk. And yes, there is a player called Hulk, he's a Brazilian forward. These two are the most powerful shooters in football right now.

Both guys are well-built and brutal with their shots. They are well-known in the soccer world to the extent that they create fear wherever they go.

Those who fear them the most are goalkeepers and defenders. If you faced any of them you would understand why this is.

There's also Hakan Calhanoglu, who plays for Turkey and Bayer Leverkusen. Calhanoglu is one of the best free kick takers in Europe at the moment.

He's also the best long distance free kick taker in the world. Back when he used to play for Hamburg, he once scored a wonderful goal against Borussia Dortmund. This was from a free kick a few meters above the center line.

For him, a free kick is like a penalty. He's so good at them that defenders panic whenever he gets a free kick against their side.

Watch the way the defenders of F.C. Köln look before he scored a goal against them. After watching that clip you will realize just how good he is at taking fouls from any distance on the field.

Shooting unpredictable balls

Sometimes there will be unexpected balls. These may be where the ball rebounds from the ground or deflects off other players. Practice these situations too. This will prepare you better for any ball that reaches you from anywhere in any way.

24. Not Being Good at Crosses and Long Passes

You will always have to know how to send quality crosses to your teammates. This applies to whatever position you play on the field. But it is especially important if you play as a right or left back.

When sending a cross, do not just aim the ball at your offensive teammate. You must shoot it so that it reaches him in a way that makes it easier for him to control and score with.

A well thought out cross will be harder for the other team's keeper and defensive players to respond to with any great effect. In brief, your crosses should be accurate, quick and dangerous.

Before looking at the necessary qualities in any detail, I want to first highlight two of the most talented defenders in the history of soccer. The first is Dani Alves (Brazil and Barcelona).

He's one of the most successful and most talented right backs of the last 20 years. Alves has three champion's league titles under his belt. The second defender I want to highlight is Ashley Cole. Many soccer experts consider him to be the best left back in the history of English soccer.

Both Alves and Cole are great examples of modern defenders who play the perfect game. They achieve this in both the attacking and the defensive sides.

Cole was part of Arsenal's invincible team. It was the only side in England to win the premier league without a single loss. Worth mentioning too, is that Ashley Cole is the only right back who has managed to keep Cristiano Ronaldo in check.

It's true; he's outshone Ronaldo in almost every game they've played against each other. Ronaldo, voted best player in the world three times, usually outperforms all rival defenders, but not Cole.

And as for Dani Alvez, he was part of the best squad ever to play for Barcelona. His fantastic performances on the right back helped him win nine European titles over eight years. These two backs should be the role models that you look to when playing on any side of the field.

Rules for Playing Crosses

Accuracy

Your cross should be easy for your teammate to translate into a goal. If not a goal, your cross should at least present him with opportunity to do something useful with the ball.

This means your cross should never fall behind your teammate. If he misses it, an opponent will probably get to steal it away.

It's also a good idea to aim the cross a little away from your teammate, to one side. This will allow him a short run at the ball, thus giving him the chance to kick it with extra force.

Where you send the cross will obviously depend on the situation at the time. Always keep in mind that your teammate should go and meet the cross rather than receive it. The reason is that he has more opportunity/momentum when he takes a few steps to get the ball.

Force the Keeper to Stay in His Position

You cross a soccer ball when you pick out a player in the goal box that can score or assist a score. Unless your teammate is waiting for your cross at the near post, keep it well away from the goal area.

It's better to keep crosses away from the goal area that you play from the sides. This will ensure the goalkeeper stays on or near to his goal line.

If he runs out at your teammate, that will only put added pressure on him. This would probably result in him taking action sooner than he'd like to.

Your cross should also be fast. This way you reduce the time the goalkeeper has to prepare himself for saving the ball. A fast cross may also tempt the keeper to leave his goal and go after the ball.

If he misses it, his goal becomes empty, leaving an opportunity for your teammate to score with a header. Remember, the most effective cross is fast and curvy (back-spinning). It is also between the six yard line and the penalty kick sign.

The quality of the cross depends on the quality of the run, or the one second acceleration, as I call it.

The one second acceleration is a crucial skill. It can help you a lot when dealing with aggressive defenders.

It is even more effective when you play against defenders who are strong, heavy and hopefully slow.

The One Second Acceleration

When dealing with strong defenders you need to have the ability to accelerate quickly. It will mean you can move from the standing still position to your fastest sprint in the blink of an eye.

This is the only way you will escape any tough defender marking you. It also gives you the momentum needed to gain the power necessary to make your cross fast and dangerous.

Like all skills, once you have developed your acceleration you still need to maintain it. There are exercises and techniques that can help you work on this.

Explosive leg exercises like frog jumps and box jumps will do a great job. If you have the chance, see if you can train alongside other sprinters. Taking tips and inspiration from these guys will encourage you to push your limits like nothing else.

Avoid sending low crosses when there are too many players in the penalty area.

Only play crosses along the ground in certain situations. You can make a low cross in counter-attacks, when there are only one or two rival defenders around to clear the ball.

When playing a low cross, the emptier the penalty area is, and the closer you are to it, the more dangerous your low cross becomes to the rival side.

Always keep a low cross away from the goalkeeper. Play them from diagonal angles rather than parallel to the goal line or inside the goal area. Never give the goalkeeper a chance to come out of his goal to grab your low cross.

Play low crosses to attackers coming from behind.

The most effective low crosses are those you send to attackers coming from behind. Rival defenders won't be aware of them and the keeper will have no chance to come out for the ball.

Practice targeted long passes to anywhere on the field.

Sometimes you will have to send long passes to create counter attacks. This is most likely when you receive the ball after a corner against your team.

Below are some exercises to help you master the skill of sending long, accurate passes to your attacking teammates.

If you can, grab one of those wooden frames your team uses for setting the wall before playing fouls. This is to substitute a teammate.

OK, place your wooden frame, or other visible object, at the other end of the field. Now kick the ball hard, and direct it so that it lands only a few inches from the wooden frame.

Repeat this drill about 100 times. Don't move the frame to a new position until you complete at least 5-10 successful passes.

Once you're good with the exercise above, it's time to move on to step two. This time, place another wooden frame or other visible object at the other side of the field.

What you're doing here is increasing your options. It means you have to decide which way to play the ball for the counter attack.

Once you've completed step two, try to then play long passes using your weak foot. This will give you a variety of options to choose from.

By using your weaker foot you get to send a more dangerous ball. This will make it easier for your teammate to receive the ball from anywhere on the field.

25. Not Being Good at Corners and Air Plays "Offensively"

Earlier in the book I discussed the explosive jump and showed you how to develop and maintain it. Below are four rules to follow. These will help you to score headers using explosive jumps.

Mastering these skills will give you an edge over the other players. Having the ability to handle crosses, high through balls and set pieces will get you noticed.

Once you get good at these things, you become an important part of the team. With these abilities, you can add new tactics and new plays into your game style.

There will be plenty of times when your team is up against a strong rival side. Their players will be challenging and perhaps depend on long balls and set pieces.

In these situations your team's strategy will need someone who is able to deal with such players in both a defensive and an offensive capacity.

If your attacking teammates are not so good at air plays, the presence of a skilled defender who is might be the solution and get your side the points they need.

Earlier in the book we looked at how to improve and maintain your explosive jump capability. There are four rules to follow which will enable you to put your jumps into practice.

When you follow these rules, you will get to score impressive goals with your header shots.

1. Take a few steps to the front.

Always take a few quick steps toward the ball when you can. This is a much better approach than just waiting for it to reach you.

If you're quick, you will get to the ball before any other player from the opposite team. Taking a few steps toward the ball will also allow you to create more energy to strike it hard with your head.

Remember, when you run toward the ball you will approach it diagonally in the penalty area.

2. Use your forehead when shooting in the same direction as your movement.

If you want to send the ball in the same direction as your run, use your forehead to strike it. This is far more effective than using the sides of your head.

Try to also keep the ball in a straight line and direct it in a slight upward direction. This allows you to send a strong ball at a lethal height (mid-range and above).

A shot like this is difficult for the keeper to save, especially if you get the right speed and the right height.

3. Lean forward when playing a side header.

There will be times when you want to send the ball in the opposite direction of your run. In these cases, lean forward and use the side of your head to strike it in the direction you want it to go.

When you head the ball at an angle like this, it is far more effective than a strong kick with the foot. And if you can, combine the shot with both speed and direction to make it even more dangerous.

The important thing to keep in mind here is to avoid directing the ball toward your shoulders or hands. That might sound easy but believe me, this happens a lot.

4. If you can't play the ball at an angle, bounce it off the ground.

There will be occasions when you intuitively know the goalkeeper is in a good position to deflect or save the ball. In these situations try to send him a bouncy header instead of a more direct shot.

If you head the ball toward the ground, it will change direction and hopefully confuse him. The secret behind a successful bouncy header is to aim the ball at the middle ground. That is, the space between you and the goalmouth, or close to it.

If you bounce the ball on the ground to close to yourself, it will lose power. Furthermore, it won't reach enough height to trick the goalie.

And when you bounce the ball too close to the goal line, it will still be powerful but it won't go high enough to make it a difficult save. So the best way by far is to aim for the middle ground every time; somewhere between you and the goal line.

26. Not Being Good at Penalty Kicks

The best penalty taker in England is a defender named Leighton Baines. Baines, who is 30 years old, has been playing for Everton for the past eight years.

He is the second best scoring defender in England, after John Terry. And he's the number one penalty taker in the English international team. He even comes before Wayne Rooney on the penalty taking list of England's greatest.

Baines has only ever missed one penalty in his ten years of playing in domestic championships. Those tournaments are the English League, the FA Cup, and the League Cup.

His one and only missed penalty happened in 2015, in a game against Manchester United. In that game, United's goalkeeper, David de Gea, managed to save Baines' late penalty, much to the surprise of many.

Because Baines is famous as a penalty taking superstar, he's in high demand in the virtual world too. Anyone playing the *Fantasy Premier League game will choose him to take their penalties every time.

Anyone who follows English soccer knows of his excellent reputation for scoring penalties. He's also a force to be reckoned with when he takes free kicks.

* *The "Fantasy Premier League game" is the official online Fantasy Football game of the Premier League. It has over three million players at the time of writing. In fact, Fantasy Premier League is the biggest Fantasy soccer game in the world right now, and best of all is that it's free to play. You can also win some great prizes if you get good. To get started, you pick your squad, create and join leagues and select your team each week.*

When the Team's Captain Slips

Remember John Terry who we talked about earlier in the book. Despite his wonderful goal scoring skills, Terry isn't a particularly good penalty shooter. Let's take the incident of 2008 to illustrate. It was when Chelsea met Manchester United in the UEFA Champions league final.

Terry was preparing to take the final penalty. On his run-up, he slipped just as he was taking the shot. This failed attempt was Chelsea's final opportunity to win. If Terry had succeeded, they would have won their first ever Champions league title.

It was devastating for the Chelsea side and their fans to see the team captain blunder like this. After all, they had put so much faith in him, hoping he would help lead them to victory in their first major trophy. It is one of those awful memories that every Chelsea fan would love to forget, but can't.

Sometimes in a penalty shootout, the teams fail to finish the game from the first five penalties. When this happens, the shootout continues on until the tenth or the eleventh penalty.

In a situation like this, you might have to take a penalty yourself, even if you're not good at it. It is a written soccer rule that you can't escape from.

This means you must know how to take a good penalty. You have to be well-prepared so that you can contribute to a shootout if need be. So you must practice shooting penalties just like any other team player.

That doesn't mean practicing only every now and again, but on a regular basis. Remember, even if you get good at something, you can't hold on to it unless you maintain the skill. And the only way to maintain a skill is through regular practice.

If you are a team captain, you will usually find yourself on the list of the first five penalty shooters. Even if you're not the captain, and you don't know how to shoot a penalty, you can still find yourself on that list.

This is why you should always be ready, willing and able to take a penalty. Your teammates need to know that they can rely on you with confidence if you ever get called upon to take a late penalty.

How to Perfect Your Penalty Kick

To score a penalty, you need two things. The first is the right mentality and the second is the right technique. Let's look at these in turn.

The Right Mentality

When taking a penalty, what you think might happen will more than likely materialize. This even applies if you're playing against an average goalkeeper. So if you think the wrong thoughts, you can't expect to succeed.

To get that ball into the net, you have to have faith in yourself that you can do it. If you carry any self-doubt around in your head, your chances of success will diminish. A famous quote by Henry Ford sums this up nicely"

"Whether you think you can do a thing, or you think you can't - you're right."

There are some techniques that will keep any self-doubts out of your head when you take a penalty, or in the lead up to it.

One is to visualize the ball smashing into the back of the net. For this to work you need to keep this image in your mind for the entire penalty taking process. If you lose focus, you can lose your chance to score.

In high stress situations like this, it's easy for self-doubt to control your thoughts. This is why you have to protect yourself against it and replace bad thinking with good. If you can maintain a strong, positive visualization, it should work like magic.

Visualization Works

Visualization does work. It is often the key to achieving what you want. It's no secret that visualization can be a powerful tool, and not only for soccer players, but for anyone, and in all areas of life. Professional athletes are very aware of the beneficial effects of this mind technique.

By using your imagination to see yourself succeed often translates to just that. This is more than just pure fantasy, it is not day dreaming, it is a proven science.

It makes perfect sense when you think about it. I mean, we can fail at something simply by having negative thoughts, so the opposite has to also be true.

The more stinking thinking you let into your head, the more negative effect it will have on your outcome.

The other way to keep negativity at bay is to use the outside distraction technique. This is useful for good penalty shooters who get jittery while waiting around for their turn.

You could, for example, think about what you're going to eat for dinner later. Or you might prefer to focus on something physical to take your mind off the pending penalty.

This could be the banners behind the goal, or the fans, as two examples. It doesn't matter where you put your focus as long as it takes your mind off the penalty. All you are doing here is distracting yourself until it's your turn to take a penalty.

Sometimes, rival players will try to distract you and make you even more nervous as you wait. Being able to block out bothersome, unwanted distraction is fundamental to your success. Basketball players actually work at blocking out distractions.

There is this unusual approach they use when they practice free throws. What they do is have someone try to distract them with a whistle or a buzzer, or even a slight hit.

The idea is to become super-focused on the task at hand. In other words, you're oblivious to anything else that's going on around you. If you're prone to outside distractions, then I urge you to practice something like this too.

Blocking Outside Distractions

When you practice your penalty taking, ask a teammate to blow a whistle right next to you. Don't worry if you don't have a whistle, use whatever you can.

He might also stand in the corner of your eye jumping up and down, waving his arms and shouting obscenities. This will more than likely annoy you at the start. If it does, then that's good.

It means you get to see how sensitive you are to distraction. You at least get a starting point from where you can get to work. It's easy to see how you progress too.

Practice this often, and don't stop until you can block out all external distractions. You might get good real quick, or it might take some time.

Either way, just stick at it until you know how to handle distractions. The time will come when you will be able to take well-focused penalties no matter what is going on around you.

The Right Technique

There are three types of shooting that have the highest probability of success. Mastering them will give you a real advantage.

It means you get to choose the right type of shot for the given situation. Being good at all three will definitely help to maintain your confidence levels.

Each of these three shots will need a fair bit of training if you're to master them well.

The first of them is perhaps the hardest of all. For this technique to work you will have to keep your eyes firmly on the keeper's legs.

You then run toward the ball, and then slow down a little just before you strike it. The idea is to wait for the goalkeeper to reveal the direction of his dive. Once he does, you kick the ball hard toward the opposite side. Of course, this all happens in nanoseconds.

The trick with this approach is all in the run-up to the ball. You slow down just before you get to it, but without stopping completely. In fact, it's against the rules to stop completely.

If you do stop, the referee will disqualify your goal, if it goes in. Instead, you will have to run, slow down, and then play the ball in the opposite direction of the keeper's movement. It's all about split second timing, that's why it's so difficult.

The second technique is to bend your body as you take the starting position. The idea behind this is to force the keeper to think what you want him to think. In this case, you want him to assume he knows which side you intend to, or appear to anticipate, sending the ball.

If you have done a good job, the keeper will be ready to dive to the left or right side of the goal. It all depends which side you lead him to believe you'll shoot at. Then, as you take the shot, you kick the ball hard toward the middle area of the goal, at mid to high range.

The most important tip here is to avoid shooting the ball on or low to the ground. This is because even if the keeper dives in a certain direction, his legs are still in the middle area of the goal. That means there is still a chance that his legs could block a low shot.

So remember to always keep your penalties away from ground level. I would say always aim at the middle height of the goal, or above it. This way, the goalie has no opportunity to stop the ball with his legs.

The third type of penalty shot is the one preferred by Cristiano Ronaldo. Here you aim at the inside of the net, either to the right or left side.

For this to succeed you need to strike the ball hard. As long as you get enough speed, it is a very hard shot for any keeper to catch.

If you can, master all three of these successful shooting techniques. If that sounds like too much, then at least get good at two of them.

Notice how I have avoided suggesting sending the ball to the upper right or left corners. That's has nothing to do with them being ineffective. In fact, such shots can be very effective when played well.

But I have left it out because it's risky and will need too much practice before you get to perfect it. As a defender, you need to focus on many other skills, not only penalties. This is why I have suggested the three easier techniques above.

You may have heard of Arturu Vidal. He's actually one of the most successful penalty takers in European soccer right now.

He rarely scores a penalty that isn't in the top corners of the goal. Most of his penalties are lethal no matter how good the keeper might be.

Watch and Learn from the Penalty Masters

I recommend you learn penalty shooting techniques by watching videos of professional penalty takers. We have looked at two of the greats already in this book, namely Leighton Baines and Arturo Vidal.

I also suggest you study the English legend and penalty master, Matt Le Tissier. He played for Southampton in the 1980s and 90s, spending a total of 16 years with the club.

Le Tissier was a complete player. He was an expert passer and had good vision. His ability to read the game was impressive.

He also had one of the best shooting techniques ever. Le Tissier was in fact the best penalty taker in the history of the English Premier League.

Right now, even 13 years after retiring from the Saints (Southhampton), Le Tissier still holds the highest penalty scoring ratio in the history of the premier league. He only has one wasted penalty out of the 26 he took between 1986 and 2002.

Le Tissier has a penalty ratio of 96.15%. That's better than all the other premier league legends.

This includes Thierry Henry (92 %), Alan Shearer (83.58 %) and Wayne Rooney (68.15 %). It's also better than Manchester United's wonderful trio, Roy Keane, Ryan Giggs and David Beckham.

Watch Le Tissier videos clips and pay close attention to his shooting style. He was one of the best of his time. He scores from both short and long distances with high accuracy and huge power. If you study his clips carefully you will get to learn a lot.

27. Not Having Good Ball Control

When you receive the ball you must make sure it doesn't stray too far. Good ball control is the ABC of becoming a successful soccer player.

In most situations you don't have a lot of space between you and your opponents. Of course, all opponents are ready to steal the ball from you the second you make a mistake.

That means the ball must be as close to your foot as possible. Any player who's any good makes the ball a natural extension to his foot. In other words, once he has it in his possession, it feels comfortable and in control.

Rule 1: Always direct the ball to the direction you want to take it.

You might want to send the ball into a new empty space, or direct it to a nearby teammate. It doesn't matter where you want to send it.

What matters is that you know what you want to do with that ball once you receive it. The most important thing about receiving any pass is to stay confident and prepared.

Rule 2: Always move toward the ball.

This is something we look at a lot in this book. That's because it's so important. Don't ever wait for the pass to reach you; always move toward it whenever possible.

You need to do this so that you can prevent the opponent next to you from intercepting the pass.

Going to meet the ball also gives you more space to escape your opponent.

28. Not Being Familiar with the Other Team's Playing Style

Not studying opponents before a game is one of the biggest mistakes that defenders make. Those who do study their opponents are at a much greater advantage than those who don't. It means they get to play a much smarter game on the day.

I'm not talking about game tactics here. Nor am I referring to the videos your coach makes you watch on video sessions before a game.

I'm actually talking about the tiny details. These are the patterns of mistakes that your opponent's make. Many of these things will not always be obvious, which is why you have to look out for them.

All players, and especially offensive ones, have their weak points. There will be parts of their game where they repeat the same or similar slips in certain situations. If you get to identify their points of weakness, you can use it against them on the day.

You need experience to be able to read the attack, the pass, and the through ball. Knowing how the opponent's intend to play a shot, before they even play it, is a powerful thing.

Furthermore, you have to be able to communicate and organize your defensive line. The more you know about the rival side, the better your chances are to block and stop the attacks early, before they pose any real danger.

Reading the game also includes positioning your teammates in set pieces and organizing your defense in corners. The more you know about the kick or the corner-taker, the better you can prepare your defense.

By studying your opponents before the game, you will have a better idea of how and where the corner-taker will most likely send his ball.

Learning about the rival players can make a huge difference on the way you play and the outcome of the game. It sounds like a lot to do, and in many ways it is. But if you're passionate about your position, and have a real desire to win, then you will enjoy studying the rival side.

Being able to predict where the next ball is likely to play, and to who, is a skill that only the most successful defenders have.

We have all seen how they predict a game with great accuracy. When this happens, you can be certain they have familiarized themselves with their opponents before game day.

You may have noticed how most teams and individual players rarely make dramatic changes to their style.

The majority of coaches, except for new coaches or the tactically flexible among them, follow a set formula. That is, they base their teams' tactics on the different strengths and weaknesses of their squad. Let's look at this a little closer.

Most British teams, except for a few among them, like to play highly physical soccer. These are games that depend on high balls and crosses. These teams tend to pick their main striker(s) based on their header skills.

This style of play has been rooted in English soccer for generations, and it rarely changes. Teams like Stoke City, for example, will play many crosses. This style of play requires a special approach.

If you study how they play corners and set pieces, you soon become familiar with their style and strategy. Any team that plays against Stoke City is up against at least five good players. They are strong, good at headers and above 1.88 m in height.

There are other teams that tend to rotate the ball often. I'm thinking here of Barcelona, Arsenal and Bayern Munich, to name three.

The defenders on the rival teams need to be good at predicting where the next ball will go. They also need to stick to their positions and stay compact as a unit, closing gaps in their defensive line.

Most of Chelsea's wins against Arsenal in the last ten years have come from the ability of Chelsea players to close all gaps in their defensive line.

This leaves the Arsenal players rotating the ball aimlessly in the middle. And then when the Chelsea players do strike, they steal the ball from Arsenal and score with a fast attack.

When dealing with different types of teams, you deal with different kinds of play. So this means you can't afford to be unfamiliar with their playing styles. Nor can you waste the chance to predict most of their playing patterns. Ignorance is not bliss in the competitive world of soccer.

This is the reason why you must spend time studying the team you will be playing against. Don't watch their games on video, study them. There is a distinct difference.

I can guarantee that by studying your rivals, you will have a huge advantage come game day. It will help you in all your decision making processes.

You will make the most of your decisions based on what you have learned about the team you're up against. Don't forget too, that a defender has a great field view.

This makes him the best one to notice any bluffing or change in tactics made by the rival side. An example might be when the other team's wingers switch to different sides of the field.

They may do this so that the fastest of them plays on the slowest or the weakest defender (right or left) in your team. A quick and crafty change like this can be devastating to your side if you fail to spot it and take action.

Ask a Lot of Questions

There are a few set questions below that you should ask yourself as you study soccer videos or live games. Be sure to take notes as you do. This will help you to identify various patterns during the games. This is what I mean when I say study as opposed to watch. When you study the game and its players, your mind is in a different mode.

OK, here are those questions:

- How good are they at rotating the ball, and how fast can they do it?
- Who are the fastest and slowest attackers on the team?
- Who is the best attacker at air-plays, and who is not so good? Who is the worst at positioning? And who gets easily caught out in the offside trap?
- Who has the most agility and highest fitness levels? Who gets exhausted fast, and beaten easily with speed?
- Who are the most physically challenging players? Who are least physically challenging?

- How good is the keeper at saving each of the following: high balls, corners and crosses?
- How good is the goalie at long shots? How's his ability to dive?

Study the tendencies or habits of your opponents. Get to know where they perform their plays. In corners and set pieces ask questions like:

- Where does the corner/foul taker prefer to send his balls and how?
- How fast do the team recover from their attacks OR how fast do they switch from attacking to defending?
- Who is the most skilled dribbler in the team?
- How do they position themselves in corners and set pieces? Are there any holes or gaps in their play that you can use to score?
- Is there any extra info you can pass on to your attacking players about the rival goalkeeper?
- How does the goalie deal with breakaways? Does he spread himself too quick or does he like to wait? Does he cover for long balls? How tall is he? And how can you use what you know about him for your own benefit?
- Is there any attacking pattern you can spot that they use to score goals?
- Where do the team's play makers like to send their through passes?

You want to take note of the style of the other team's key player(s). Watch how they play through-passes or send long balls.

When you familiarize yourself with these things you get to anticipate and stop lots of dangerous balls early on.

At the age of 36, key players like Andrea Pirlo will send higher through-balls from wider areas instead of running. Being aware of something like this can help you intercept long passes early on, long before any of the opponents reach them.

You will be able to find more questions that are applicable to the style of your team and the way you play. I'm sure you get the general idea though.

Once you have your "questions template" you might want to keep a file on the computer. This way you can create a new blank file for each new side you prepare to play.

This is something that will undoubtedly give you an edge on game days. Both your physical and mental game is going to get a performance boost because of your pre-game prep.

Remember to share your findings with your teammates. They should also study the team themselves.

If they have done, then you will have a pretty powerful picture built up between you all. This means there's an excellent chance of your side dominating the game on the day.

All Players Make Repeated Mistakes

As mentioned earlier, all players have their weak points, even the greats. They will make certain mistakes that they repeat over and over, despite their best efforts not to.

We've looked at Per Mertesacker problems earlier. We saw how his game deteriorated when he faced counter attacks with fast players. Now I will use Gary Cahill, the England and Chelsea center back, as another example.

Cahill is one of the best defenders in the English premier league. He was recently picked for the 2015 premier league's all-star team. Yet despite his brilliance, the man still has serious problems. His weakness is setting offside traps and dealing with counter attacks.

If you ever study Cahill's performance, you will notice how it drops whenever he's not playing next to Chelsea's captain, John Terry. Sometimes it drops by quite a bit too.

Terry, who's one of the best European defenders of the last 10 years, contributes to Cahill's game. He sets roles, completes, and often covers his teammate's mistakes.

I wouldn't go as far to say that he carries him, but Cahill is definitely not as good without Terry.

Here's another example of how a player's game can go off par when things change on the field. After Roberto Carlos retired from soccer, the Real Madrid legend confessed something.

He said he would suffer whenever the guy he was watching on the left flank went deeper inside the field and switched roles with another teammate.

During his last days in Spain, he and his team had some bad games against Barcelona. This included a 6-2 loss in the Santiago Bernabéu Stadium. It was all due to Barcelona's continuous motion and the ability of their attacking line to quickly and frequently switch roles. This is what threw Carlos off.

Just know that even though there are some great players out there, none of them is perfect. Some might be near to it, but even the best will have some area where they fall short.

So your job is to study the players on the rival sides and learn of their shortcomings. Once you get good at this you will be in much better control of your game.

29. Not Being Familiar with the Striker You're Going to Mark

OK, so let's assume you have finished your homework. You have now gotten familiar with the different tactics and playing styles of the rival team.

Your next job is to zoom in and focus in the team's key players. Pay particular attention to their main striker or the leading goal scorer.

In most teams there will be two or three key players. These are the guys who are responsible for creating and scoring 80 percent of their side's goals. These are the ones you need to focus on the most.

How to Study Key Players

The way you study the key players is by looking out for their patterns. Also look out for any little tricks they might like to use often. We all form habits, some good, others bad. Bad habits can be hard to break though, impossible sometimes. This is especially true when the pressure is on.

You see, there will be little things, quirks if you like, which are a part of who we are, no matter how hard we try to change.

All players - and I do mean all players - have something about their style that you can use to your advantage on game day. Knowing what they are good at, as well as what they're not, all counts. OK, let's start by taking a look at how to identify patterns in a player.

Player Patterns

Thierry Henry

Henry used to stand in the offside for a little longer than usual. He would wait for any pass that a rival defender would send to his teammate.

When he did, Henry would charge in and try to snatch the ball and score. Watch his goal against England in the 2004 European Cup.

In this incident he flipped the game upside down in the final minutes. What he did was intercept a pass from Steven Gerard to his keeper David James.

I was watching some highlights for Manchester United's new winger a while back. He name is Anthony Martial. They now call Martial "The New Henry." Why? Because he does the exact same thing that Henry used to do. He sneaks up behind a defender, waits for a wrong pass, and then steals the ball away at every opportunity.

Filippo Inzaghi

One of AC Milan's attacking legends, Filippo Inzaghi, had the nickname "King of the Offside Trap." This was because he would fall for the offside five or ten times during a single game, until he got his opportunity to act. His tactic was to wait until rival defenders felt safe.

When the moment was right, he'd surprise them by making a quick move at just the right moment. This would put him in a sudden one-to-one situation with their goalkeeper from where he'd often score.

Inzaghi was a goal scoring machine, but he wasn't talented, not in the usual sense. His mind was the only thing that made him one of the greatest strikers to ever play for Milan.

Arjen Robben

If you have followed the style of Arjen Robben since he played for Chelsea up till now, you will know how he can be a bit selfish. In fact, the Dutch winger can be very selfish at times.

The reason is that Robben is a ball-hogger. He will only ever pass to his fellow teammates when it's absolutely necessary. At all other times he will hold on to that ball for dear life.

The way to mark someone like Robben is to isolate them on the corner. You do this using a couple of players.

This way you get to steal the ball from him without too much difficulty. This is because anytime he tries to run with the ball, instead of passing it on, it's hard for him to win when there are two guys containing his moves.

Robben also has the habit of running along the right flank. From there he suddenly goes deeper into the field before he fires a strong shot toward the far post of the goal.

He rarely crosses and he rarely passes. This is part of his selfish style. He will try this trick whenever he finds the slightest opportunity to have a go.

Anyone who familiarizes themselves with Robben's style of play is going to have a much better chance of defeating him on the field.

From his repeated patterns you will know how and where he likes to play his balls and shots. Once you can predict his moves, you get to position yourself so that you're prepared to respond. Anyone who's unfamiliar with Robben's style of play is vulnerable to his tricks.

Arsenal's winger, Theo Walcott, is another ball-hogger. Anytime he he's trapped close to the goal area, or in a breakaway, he'd sooner play a chip over the goalkeeper rather than pass the ball to his nearest teammate.

Dennis Bergkamp

Netherlands's legend, Dennis Bergkamp, had a strange approach. He was one of those rare strikers who preferred to score from outside the penalty area.

He was the kind of attacker who would retreat to receive the ball from outside the penalty box. From there he would then send a strong shot or a lob over the goalkeeper's head.

Bergkamp is one of the few attackers who have a similar number of assists as he has goals. Again, anyone who familiarizes themselves with his style is in a much better position to defeat him on the field.

Competing against him would force a defensive midfielder to meet him early in the penalty area. From there he could prevent leaving a space for Bergkamp to work his magic. Anyone unfamiliar with his style would obviously have a lot less chance to stop him.

Eden Hazard

Eden Hazard makes a small feint anytime he decides to go deep from the flank toward the penalty area. He does this so that he can have an easier shot at the goal. Noticing such a move will give you a signal to prepare yourself because you know what's to follow. You are then in a good position to block the shot that will happen within the next few seconds.

The Conclusion

Studying team strategies and player's patterns empowers you on the soccer field. When you prepare this way you are in more control of your game. This is something you must look for if you're to be good at defending. When you take responsibility over everything that happens around you, you then get to leverage your performance. You can't afford not to study your opponent's best players before a game. If you do, even a weaker side could defeat you on the day.

30. Not Playing on the Referee's Whistle

A common mistake that happens in soccer is when a defensive player thinks he deserves a foul. In these situations he stops playing, or he stops marking an opponent.

He then stands there, waiting for the referee to give him what he wants. Unlucky for the defender, the referee allows the play to continue.

This means he either failed to see the foul or he didn't think the incident warranted one. You can see the same thing happen in a fake offside. In this case, the defenders or the goalkeeper stops playing.

Again, they just stand there and raise their hands, assuming the ref will award an indirect free kick. But he won't always do this. It then leaves the opponents with a golden opportunity to score a goal, without any distraction or resistance.

The message here is to never assume. No matter how obvious something might seem to you, you won't get to make the referees decisions for him. Until you hear that whistle, you have to play on as normal.

If you don't, then it may be to your detriment. This is even more important when the ball is inside the penalty area and you're calling for an offside or a regular free kick against your opponent.

31. Lacking Confidence

You may be a decent height and also have a strong, well-toned body. You might also have the ability to read the game. And perhaps you have the good fortune to make it into a decent team.

You are, to all intents and purposes, a "good" player. But good isn't great, it's just decent. And you will never be great at defending if you don't have a strong belief in yourself and your abilities.

The Skill of Self Confidence

In one of his TedX talks, Dr. Ivan Joseph spoke about what he looks for in a player.

For anyone who doesn't know him, Dr. Ivan Joseph is a respected university soccer coach in the USA.

He explains that the most important things he looks for first in an individual are self-confidence and self-belief. Anything else is secondary.

Whether he accepts a student and awards them scholarship depends on how they perceive themselves. For Dr. Ivan Joseph, they must have total faith and belief in their ability to succeed. Or at the very least they must have the "potential" to have total faith and belief in their ability to succeed.

Dr. Ivan Joseph defines confidence like this:

"It's the skill of believing in one's ability to perform an act or reach a desired result despite the odds, the difficulty, or the adversity."

He goes on to say that no matter how strong or how fast a player is; these physical features won't serve him or her well if the belief in one's self was absent.

He explains his idea with the following quote:

"When we lose sight or lose belief in ourselves, then we will end up achieving nothing."

I recommend you search for his TEDx speech on YouTube. Just type: Dr. Ivan Joseph - The Skill of Self Confidence – TED.

Solid Defenders Are Confident Defenders

You can measure how strong a team is by how strong its defenders are.

This applies to the two center backs in particular.

Take a look at all the strong, A-Class soccer teams that you know of. Note how 90 percent of them have a pair of defenders who have a combination of self-confidence and leadership skills.

Look at John Terry, Tony Adams, Paolo Maldini and Fernando Hierro. All these guys were center backs. They were captains too, and they all had the confidence to lead their teams to a lot of trophies.

If you don't have it, you will want to know how to build your own self-confidence as a defensive player. Those of you who have watched the video mentioned above will already know the answer.

Still, let's write these things down too, so that you have reference to them in this book as well. It comes down to two things, namely repetition and affirmations.

The Importance of Repetition

You first need to identify your mistakes and weak points. This is because they are the problem. It's impossible to apply a solution to anything until you first understand the problem.

Once you have identified your problem areas you need to zoom in and work hard at fixing them. If it's a lack of some skill, you have to work over and over until you have improved it.

When you can do something well you become confident. When you can't, you are insecure and lack confidence.

In the TEDx talk with Dr. Joseph (see above), he gives an example of one of his goalkeepers. This guy, despite being physically capable, had a problem with catching the ball.

No matter how hard he tried, the ball would almost always slip through his fingers. There was nothing wrong with his hands or his eyesight, but the more he tried, the more he failed.

What happened was that he'd convinced himself that he was useless when it came to catching a soccer ball.

Now is a good time to repeat the wise words of Henry Ford:

"Whether you think you can, or you think you can't, you're right on both counts."

It's all about what you believe to be true. Just as we can excel with the right level of confidence, so we can fail without it. Having the physical potential doesn't help if the brain is not on side.

In the case of the young goalie above, let's look at how he overcame his inability to catch soccer balls.

Under the instruction of Dr. Joseph, he practiced kicking a ball against a wall and catching it on the rebound, or at least tried to catch it.

He did this 350 times a day for eight consecutive months. Simple repetition was the method used here. So did he make it, did he overcome his belief that he was useless when it came to catching a soccer ball?

Well, let's just say he found his confidence and went on to play at a professional level in Europe. For him, what must have once seemed like an impossible dream had become his reality.

For you to duplicate this approach you first have to find out what you are not so good at. Once you do, you then get to work at fixing your weak areas using the simple repetition technique. Don't let impatience get the better of you either.

Just do the best you can for the agreed amount of training time. Whatever you do, don't tell yourself that you can't do it, or that you're no good. That kind of thinking will only hold you back still further. It's also important here to look for progress, not perfection.

Let's say you are not good at corners, for example. In this case, get someone to send you crosses from different positions and sides of the field. Do it every night if you can, or after finishing your regular training sessions.

Promise yourself that you will keep at it until you are happy and confident in your ability. It might take two or three weeks, or it might take six months or even one year. Don't worry about the time. Focus only on the task.

Tell yourself from the outset that it takes as long as it takes, and then just get on with the job in hand. You might sometimes have a bad day, or a bad few days, where nothing seems to go right.

If this happens, just remind yourself that it's all part of the process. Tell yourself that your improvement is inevitable, despite any setbacks along the way.

Perhaps you're not good at headers. In this case, get someone to send you crosses from different positions and sides of the field. Put fixed signs on the goal and point your headers toward them.

Do this every night after finishing your regular training. Keep at it for as long as it takes. With enough commitment and repetition, you will eventually feel confident at corners and with fouls.

If you are not good at penalties, get lots of repetitive practice in with these two. Again, don't give up until your skill and confidence reaches acceptable levels.

Maybe you're not good at tackling or at marking other players. What I suggest here is to train more with younger and older teams, beyond your regular training.

This will break you away from familiarity, which is a good way to challenge yourself. It also gets you some fresh feedback from others. Find out what you're bad at, ask advice on how to fix it, and then get to work.

Whatever area or areas need improvement, use the repetition technique to zoom in and focus on them. Repetition is the mother of skill.

Constant repetition carries conviction. This works, it really does work, providing that is, you stick to the plan.

Affirmations

Affirmations are positive statements that describe a desired situation. The general approach is to repeat them over and over.

This is often done out loud, until they get impressed on the subconscious mind. In other words, you repeat them until you believe them to be true.

In your case, these affirmations need to be specific statements. When practiced often they will help you to overcome self-sabotaging, negative thoughts and beliefs.

Muhammad Ali, the greatest boxer of all time, once said:

"I am the greatest. I said that before I knew I was."

And this is exactly what you should be telling yourself. Anything less and you will get less.

Belief is something that works both ways, as we have seen in the Henry Ford quote above. Just know that you are only ever able to excel in something when you believe it's achievable. Likewise, you will never be able to achieve something if you think it's impossible.

In other words, you're right on both counts. So if you believe that you are just average or mediocre, and will never be anything other than this, then you're right.

Can you identify with having self-doubts? If yes, then you will want to get some powerful and positive affirmations working for you.

Just because you don't think you can do a thing, that doesn't mean you can't. It just means you think you can't. But if you always think that way, then you will never change.

In a situation like this, you have to fake it till you make it. This not only applies to soccer, but to life in general. If you're still skeptical about this approach, my advice is simple, and that is to never knock something new until you have tried it.

If you can't do something, it is most likely because you have convinced yourself you can't. In other words, even though you don't know it, you have been using affirmations all along.

The problem is you've been telling yourself you can't do a thing. I'm sure you can now see what has been happening here.

You have been feeding your mind with negative affirmations. See, when you tell yourself something often enough, you end up believing it.

Well, positive affirmations work in the exact same way. The only difference here is that you're using affirmations for positive purpose, not negative.

To build a new belief system does not require rocket science. Whatever you repeat the most is what the subconscious mind ends up believing to be true. Don't let the simplicity of this approach deter you.

This is a technique that works, and there is scientific evidence to back this up. All kinds of people use positive affirmations to help change their life for the better. If you want changes in your own belief system, you now know how to do it.

Remember, thinking without doing won't help. By that, I mean it's no good believing you're great at goal kicks if you don't get out there and prove yourself right.

When you believe you can do a thing, then achieving it becomes so much easier. So whatever you do, remember to act on your thoughts. That's positive thoughts, not negative.

Scientists and researchers have tried to explain the phenomenon of the different mindsets. They believe it comes down to two things. One is what they call the Growth Mindset, and other is the Fixed Mindset. Let's look at each of these in turn.

The Growth Mindset

Anyone with a "growth mindset" is positive. They believe they can develop their most basic abilities through dedication and hard work.

They are generally upbeat in their attitude and outlook upon life in general. Those with a growth mindset have within them a genuine love of learning. In essence, they have a resilience that is essential for great accomplishment.

If you look at all the soccer greats, you will find that many of them have these qualities. Having a growth mindset creates motivation and productivity. This not only applies to soccer but to all sports. It applies to business and education as well.

People with this kind of mindset tend to have good relationships with their fellows. To sum up, people with a growth mindset are happier, healthier and have a real zest for living. They embrace new challenges, knowing that they will come out stronger on the other side.

The Fixed Mindset

People with a "fixed mindset" tend to think more than they act. They do believe in their basic qualities. For example, they believe in their talent, their intelligence, and their physical abilities, etc. But acknowledging their basic qualities is usually where it stops.

Despite any beliefs they may have, they do little or nothing to develop themselves further. These types dread failure so they avoid it by no trying. They feel that talent on its own is enough to succeed.

They think that some people are lucky because they are born with certain gifts. They're wrong, of course, because talent alone is never enough to succeed at anything. But their belief system is so fixed that it's hard to convince them otherwise.

People of a fixed mindset are inflexible. You've heard the saying, "stuck in his ways." Well, that is typical of a fixed mindset personality. So people of this mindset belong in the "all-talk and no-action" category.

They usually have a lowly opinion of themselves in general, even though they might not voice it out loud. They worry too much about their traits.

With a fixed mindset it's hard to deal with criticism, even when it's constructive. In short, a fixed mindset suggests limited negative thinking patterns.

If you can identify as having a fixed mindset then don't get too despondent. You can change your conviction through various exercises.

In fact, there have been entire books written on the subject. But to sum it up in brief, here is the crux of what you need to do to shift from a negative, fixed mindset, to a positive, growth mindset.

Listen to Your Fixed Mindset "Voice"

Learn to listen to your fixed mindset "voice." This is the voice that tells you that something is impossible.

It is the voice that says you can't do a thing. It then justifies itself by having you come up with 101 reasons why this is true.

So the first thing to do is to recognize this voice. Understand that YOU are not your mind. Your mind is a part of who you are, just like any other body part. That means you can learn to control it.

Acknowledge Your Choices

The second thing to do is to acknowledge the fact that you have choices. So far you have chosen to believe a lot that is negative.

It is something that you often do at the subconscious level. You can now choose not to believe your fixed-mindset at the conscious level.

From today, you get to choose to develop your growth-mindset. Whenever your inner voice tells you, "No, you can't," turn things around by saying, "Oh yes I can."

Listen, Learn and Act

Finally, practice at hearing both voices, fixed and growth. Get used to taking (choosing) the growth mindset action. For example, say you're having a tough time diving.

The old fixed mindset might tell you that it's because you've reached the limits of your potential. It tells you that this is as good as you're likely to get, so QUIT trying to improve.

And your growth mindset tells you there's lots of room for improvement. It suggests you look at other ways to develop, and maybe you could ask for help from those more experienced. You choose to listen to the growth mindset and take fresh action.

To begin with, your fixed mindset will be your default way of thinking. You will have to counteract it by forcing the growth mindset to take part. What you're doing here is trying to wake up the growth mindset.

Just start by giving yourself alternative options. These are usually the total opposite to what the fixed mindset suggests. So if your fixed mindset says, "No, you can't," replace that with "Yes I can, and I will." I'm sure you get the idea.

You must remember to always take positive action on positive thoughts. If you get into the habit of doing this, your growth mindset will eventually take over from the fixed one. This is something that may take a while, depending on how fixed your mindset has become. So the sooner you start, the quicker you get to transform.

If you need more help, there are plenty of good books and articles online that will guide you through this process.

32. Not Having a Fixed Visualization Routine

Before we get started, let's be clear on two things:
1. If you can't dream it, you won`t get it.
2. All great players are into visualization.

We've already touched on visualization earlier in the book. All the same, this is so important and so powerful that it deserves a chapter of its own. Soccer players who practice visualization are more successful than those who don't.

There are two main reasons to perform visualization. One is that it prepares you so that you can perform at your best. The other is that it takes no effort, money, or resources. Let's look at these in more detail.

Visualization Prepares You

When done well, visualization helps to prepare you for the game ahead. Because of this, you get to perform better on the field.

You predict certain scenarios and are ready for whatever new happens to you or to your team during the game. Anytime you visualize yourself performing well, something special happens on game day.

You help your brain to identify and remove many obstacles. These are things that might have otherwise gotten in your way if you hadn't visualized them beforehand.

Visualization also enhances your decision making process. It makes you faster and more accurate when you have to weigh up your options. Your reflexes become quicker too. This is because you have already practiced and anticipated various situations inside your mind.

Visualization Is Easy

Visualization won't exhaust you. In fact, the opposite is true, it will relax you. It is something that you can do anytime and anywhere. It takes no energy, physical or emotional, and so it won't leave you feeling any kind of fatigue.

I would say that there is no simpler way to increase your success than to visualize it. The sheer simplicity of this approach puts a lot of people off though. They think that it's just too good to be true, and so they write it off as some kind of hoax.

They still think this way despite having the science there to back up the effectiveness of this technique. All I know is that anyone who is resistant to visualization techniques are missing out big time.

Like I said earlier, it's never a good idea to knock something until you try it. And when it comes to visualization, there's nothing to lose but a bit of your time.

The famous Man United attacker, Wayne Rooney, uses visualization. In an interview once, he revealed that his visualization routine has helped him score many great goals.

And Rooney has scored a lot of stunning goals in his time. You should be able to find them easy enough in video sharing websites like YouTube.

Rooney would spend the whole night before the game visualizing events on the field. He would be playing in the exact kit he'd be wearing on the day, and performing well against the opposition. He would score some great goals for his side and make some impressive moves.

Rooney said that his reason behind doing visualization was simple. It was so that he could mentally prepare for every single situation he may face during the actual game. He said it acted as his "game memory." His "game memory," as he called it, were the last visualizations embedded into his mind.

Rooney said that visualization helped him to score some of the most amazing goals early on in his career too. It helped him to hit far posts from 30 yards, and sometimes further.

He also got to perform Messi type tricks, like dribbling through numerous opponents in a single play. None of this, he thinks, would have been possible without visualization.

So powerful is visualization, that soccer players and athletes from around the world use it as an integral part of their strategy. They do this because it's easy and effective, and that's about it.

You get to translate your positive visualizations into positive actions on the field. Visualization doesn't need much for it to become effective. I would suggest something like 20-30 minutes a day, and maybe twice that time the night before game day.

This is not a case of day dreaming or fantasizing. What you are doing is envisaging how real events might play out. You then visualize how you intend to deal with them if they materialize. Visualizations are always positive and you are always the star of the show.

Before you start your visualization sessions, make sure you know what your goals are. Write stuff down beforehand if need be. Once you know how you need to perform in various situations, sit back, relax, and play them over in your head.

The Importance of Clarity

Visualization provides you with clarity. This clearness of mind enables you to unleash latent skills and capabilities. It helps you to focus your attention, your energy, and your time on the important things.

With clarity you get to track and process everything around you. This means you can avoid all obstacles as you are able to see things from a higher perspective. Visualization is the most empowering mind-technique for any player wanting to improve his game.

Successful people, from all walks of life, use visualization on a regular basis. They do not use it in the hope that it will work, they practice it because it does work.

It provides them with clarity, something which is lacking in today's busy world. It's true, modern lifestyles have stripped us of this once common quality.

In fact, too many distractions in life kill the dreams of many aspiring soccer players. This is why it's so important to clear the clutter from the mind and replace the space with clear, simple focus.

Twenty-first century living and lifestyles has left many of us with a limited focus span. Every single day things move on, cease to be, or get changed.

It seems impossible to focus on anything for too long at a time. One moment you place your focus on one thing and the next on something else.

Heck, it's no wonder that stress has become the curse of this new millennium. For all these reasons and more, you need to see your goals before you achieve them.

You have to hardwire your game plan into your mind, and visualizations help you to do just that. With clarity comes the elimination of chaos, confusion and turmoil.

It's time to put a stop to all the everyday stuff that gets in the way. It's time to step back from the usual routine and ignite your focus. It's time to visualize what you want so that you can get it.

Remember, your hopes and dreams to excel at soccer will always be just hopes and dreams without a plan.

The only way to get what you want is with real clarity, and that is something you can claim with visualization.

33. Not Knowing How to Deal with a Counter Attacks

It's crucial that you know how to contain an attacker. This is especially important when you become outnumbered or are involved in a counter attack.

The best way to do this is to force the attacker to move toward the side line. This approach is much better than letting him go deep inside the penalty area or to its edge.

OK, let's look at how to achieve this.

- Position yourself in a way that blocks all possible passes or predicted runs.

- Ask for help from another teammate. You are the one who puts the pressure on while your teammate waits to intercept the pass. Your teammate should be vigilant in these situations. He must get the ball because losing it here could pose serious danger to your goal. This is even more important if there is no one on your team guarding the goal area.
- If you're not sure whether you'll take the ball, pause for a brief moment. In these situations let the attacker come to you. If you get out of the game and he passes you, it's almost a breakaway.
- Be willing to cover for any player when needed. For example, a long through pass gets played toward the side of your penalty area and your center back decides to go after the ball. His hope is to pressure the ball holder on the flank. By doing this he leaves an empty spot in the penalty area. What should you do? You should cover his back without hesitation and take his position inside the penalty area. Wait there for any cross that comes your way in case he fails to get the ball from the opposite attacker.
- If a player runs behind you and waits for the ball, just forget about him. Focus instead on the player that faces you.
- Never take your eyes off the ball. Focus on it instead of the attacker's legs. Remember, it's the ball you`re after not his foot.

- Always prepare yourself for a tackle. Don't ever be afraid to send the ball outside the field for a throw-in or a corner if need be. It's better this way than conceding a goal.
- If you already have a yellow card, stick to your position and let a teammate with a clear sheet go after the attacker. After all, he may have to make a foul against the opponent. That is something you can't afford to do with your one yellow card.
- Be responsive with your feet and prepare to close them in an instant. This is because the top way of moving past a LB or RB is to send the ball between his legs.
- Watch videos for the rival winger before the game. See how he deals with defenders in counter attacks so that you can prepare better for his style of play.
- When tackling or sliding, make sure you touch the ball before the opponent does. This is so that he doesn't get a foul or a penalty.
- Don't slide unless you're in the perfect position to reach the ball with ease. Sliding for the sake of it can cause you a lot of unnecessary problems.
- If the player attacks you from the flank and you see his teammate coming from behind to receive his cross, stop this cross at all cost.
- Just know that the more determined you are to get the ball, the better your chances will be of extracting it.

34. Not Considering
Becoming the Best

Four key players form the base of every great team. They consist of a strong goalkeeper, a sneaky attacker, a tough defender midfielder, and a solid defender.

Give any coach these four to work with and he can do miracles. During his later days at Man United, Sir Alex Furguson managed to win league titles with a group of average players. There were even times when he had to play with below average players.

He could do this because he still put together a good top four on the team. The guys he had at his disposal were: Edwin Van der Sarr (GK) Rio Ferdinand and Vidic (CB). He also had Michael Carrick (DM) and Ruud van Nisterlory/Wayne Rooney.

So why am I mentioning this?

Because I want you to realize that A–class defenders are both rare and valuable. Big teams pay big money for having any of these guys.

You can judge a team's performance and their ability to win trophies and championships by knowing who plays on its defensive line. You can do this even before you look at their attacking options.

Many teams have ordinary and average strikers yet still go on to win trophies. They can do this because of their solid defensive line.

The difference between successful and unsuccessful coaches is simply down to how they put their teams together. The good ones, like Jose Mourinho, will always secure the team's goal before considering their scoring strategy.

Average goals lead to average actions and eventually, an average life.

Don't allow your goals to be shallow and limited.

You don't want to just play for some team, make some money, and buy some nice things. You can achieve stuff like that with a normal 9-5 job. Instead you should aim as high as your mind can take you.

Set goals bigger than you can imagine and have very high expectations of yourself. The most important thing of all is to always put soccer first. It should always be about the game, above all the spoils that a successful career may bring with it.

It is only when you set big goals that you get to excel. Anything less and you will get less. The most successful players never reached greatness by dreaming average dreams.

If you want remarkable success, set your sights on exceptional targets. When you truly believe in your ability to reach greatness anything is possible.

Still not convinced? OK, it's time to introduce you to the 10X way of thinking.

The 10X Rule

This has to be one of the best books ever written about success and attaining a winning mindset. The 10X Rule is a book by an American Multimillionaire salesman called Grant Cardone.

I have read this book cover to cover many times in the past and will continue to re-read it. I recommend that you do the same.

Don't worry; this isn't just another self-help book from some self-confessed inspirational coach. This is a motivational and practical program for success. It is far better than anything else I have ever read.

Grant Cardone teaches the real principles of self-belief. If you need a motivational boost then this is the book for you.

It is a fresh approach that will inspire you to raise your standards so that you can go on to achieve greater things. This is the only book you will ever need to deal with motivational issues.

I recommend that you read and reread this book until the principles of the 10X Rule embed deep inside your mind.

When this happens, the way you think, feel, and function will change forever. After you have read it through once or twice you will understand why so many people call this "The Encyclopedia of Success."

Any great soccer player has to develop his mindset if he's to excel in his position. The 10X Rule can help you to do just that.

Apply the advice from this book into your own life and watch how it changes. You will go on to develop a winning attitude like the players Cristiano Ronaldo and Wayne Rooney. You will get to remove any self-doubts that have hindered you up until now.

Quite often, the only thing that blocks us from greatness are the obstacles created in our minds. The way we think affects the way we feel and the way we function. If you can think and believe in great things then great things will come to pass.

Let me tell you something about the Grant Cardone approach to give you a flavor of his teaching. The main and most important method in this book is the idea of aiming high, very high. You start off by setting yourself huge goals. These goals should be way beyond any targets you have set before.

You might already be thinking that this is an unrealistic approach draped in fantasy. I know I did at first. And if you know my work, you also know how I always talk of the importance of setting "realistic" goals.

But when I talk about being "realistic," I am referring to the mini goals, or checkpoints along the way. These are the small targets used as stepping stones to the main, bigger goal. They are not the end goals, which should always be set high.

Having ambitious goals is vital for success. They are what push and motivate you to take more actions and achieve better results. This all sounds logical enough, yet there is a common setback among many.

The problem is that a lot of people never aim high enough. Because of this, they restrict themselves from realizing their full potential. Maybe you can relate to this too.

Whether you know it or not, you will have some self-doubt, to a greater or lesser degree. You must release yourself from the shackles of this curse.

It is only when you become free of self-doubt that you get to excel beyond your wildest dreams. This is where the 10X Rule comes to your rescue.

The author of the 10x rule suggests you make your goals huge. That means 10, 20 or even 50 times bigger than the ones you had set previous. It might sound ridiculous, but it's not. The most ridiculous thing is the silly little goals that most people set for themselves. This is why there are more foot soldiers in society than winners and leaders.

Cardone also suggests using smaller, more achievable goals as a way to reach your main target. This is a logical and workable approach.

Because your end goal is now much bigger and a lot grander, you will be keen to get there as soon as you can. This means your mini goals will also be more ambitious.

Your smaller goals still need to be achievable, but they also need to be challenging. By making them a little tough, your efforts will intensify.

Small, mediocre, easy-to-achieve goals only result in mediocre progress. It's this lackluster approach that so often blocks a person's ability to excel.

OK, let's use an entrepreneurial scenario as a way to illustrate these points.

Imagine that you want to build a new company for yourself. Your main goal with this new venture is to generate a decent income. Now, which of the following would you prefer to end up with for your efforts? [1] A company worth $500,000 USD? [2] A company worth $100,000,000 USD? It doesn't take a genius to guess your answer. Of course you would want a successful $100,000,000 dollar company.

So you set yourself a genuine goal to make a $100m company. Obviously you will have a much different mindset than if you had planned to build a smaller business. So as you proceed, the chances are that you will be aggressive, ambitious and driven. You will have a lot more of each of these things than if you settled on creating a company worth $500,000 USD.

Here's something to think about:

If you set yourself a low goal, it is unlikely that you will ever exceed it. Put another way, if you believe you are only able to achieve something up to a certain level, you are right.

Most people only dream about doing great things, or becoming what others have become. The dreaming stage is where most ambitious plans stop for many.

In other words, dreamers do little more than fantasize about greatness. They don't believe their dreams could ever come true, not for them, and so they never do.

If someone believes they can never become any better than they are, that doesn't mean they can't. It just means they think they can't, and they're right too, they can't.

It's not possible to come to much when they place such restrictions on themselves. The only way out of this mindset is to unleash the real potential that lies within. And the only way to do that is to change their belief system.

Any great soccer player will tell you that they always set themselves high goals. If they didn't, they would never get to develop their skills to the levels they reach.

The only reason they can aim high is because they have a genuine belief in themselves. This is the only way that they can get to where they want to go.

Even as young, enthusiastic players who were a long way off their dreams, they still held onto their beliefs. If they didn't believe, then they would never have made the grade. Talent alone is futile without positive action.

If you want to be up there with the world's best defenders, then that has to be your end goal. Anything less and you will fall short. That is something I can guarantee.

The next time you play with your team, set a higher standard for yourself. In every game aim to play even better than you did in the game before it.

If you just turn up and hope you'll do okay on the day, then your ability to excel will always lie dormant. Take this "higher goal" approach in everything that you do. That includes training sessions too.

Always strive to excel beyond anything you have hoped for in the past. Maintain your focus and never settle for anything less than greatness. Don't worry if you fall short, because you will at times, perhaps on many occasions.

The point is to learn from any failures and never ever lower the bar. So aim high, and continue to aim high and great things will materialize as long as you believe they will.

Remember to never let any setbacks influence you in a negative way. Just shrug them off as mere blips and keep moving forward.

A winning mentality is what creates champions. This has to be your new mindset. This is the way to think and believe. You need to hardwire this into your psyche.

It is how big teams win big games and take home big trophies. For example, look at a dominant team like Bayern Munich, and a dominant coach like Guardiola.

They enter each game with the aim of coming away with more than just three points. They are always hungry for more, and they always want to score 7-8 goals per game.

In fact, Bayern Munich is the only team in Europe to have the highest number of goals scored per game. They do all this without the luxury of star players on their side like the goal scoring machines Messi and Ronaldo.

Only you can determine your success. You have to fall in love with the dream. You must give it the required effort to turn it into a reality. Change the way you view yourself and your potential, and positive changes will materialize.

You need to ask yourself a simple question. Is better for you to take actions toward the goal of becoming one of the best 10 players in your position, in the whole world, or to aim for only being the best player in your team, or your league?

Setting the latter goals is easy and won't need you to exert too much effort. If you aim for the sky, you force yourself to develop a much stronger work ethic. Physical talent needs positive thoughts if it's to be of any use to you.

Never forget, the way you think affects the way you feel about things. And the way you feel affects the way you perform. These things are all interconnected. Once you get your brain into the right gear, the body will follow.

I believe you are already motivated. You might need to be more motivated, but you have already planted the seeds of success. I assume this because you have bought this book so that you can improve your game.

35. You Don`t Have Enough Muscle

You won't ever reach a high level of physical endurance, agility and speed with a weak body. This is especially true when playing as a defensive midfielder. The position needs you to make a lot of tackles in each game, often against players who will be bigger and stronger than you are.

There are a few players who are not physically solid and lack muscle. Arsenal's Francis Coquelin is one of them. He's actually only about 74 kg. Even so, this type of player is the exception not the rule.

Let's look at some other players and see how their lack of muscle and strength became their biggest setback.

Eduardo Da Silva

Eduardo Da Silva, commonly known as Eduardo, is a Brazilian-born Croatian attacker. He played for Arsenal between the years 2007 and 2010.

He was one of the most skilled strikers I have ever seen. This is not just my opinion but that of many Arsenal fans too.

In fact, his coach, Arsene Wenger, believed he was one of the best strikers to ever play in the English club.

This could have made him a club legend, but it wasn't to be. This is because Eduardo's career had a major setback.

He was the type of striker any soccer fan would love to see play for their team. Eduardo was fast, he was smart, and he always knew where to position himself when he played at Arsenal. Best of all is that he knew how to finish.

He was a great player, that's for sure, but I say "was" for a reason. You see, Eduardo had a major setback in that he wasn't solid and strong, making him too fragile for the game.

In his first 27 games with Arsenal, Eduardo had scored 19 goals for the team. Besides this, he also had 12 assists to add to his sheet. Then, one day the inevitable happened.

Eduardo suffered a sickening injury in a league game against Birmingham City. The incident happened when City player, Martin Taylor, broke Eduardo's leg.

It was in fact, one of the most shocking incidents in the history of the English premier league. Without going into too much detail, Taylor caught Eduardo on the shin.

As they collided, Taylor snapped Eduardo's fibula. The fibula is the outer of the two bones between the knee and the ankle. He also dislocated his left ankle.

Because of his injuries, Eduardo had no choice but to spend almost an entire year in the hospital. The medical team had a lot of work to do if they were to prepare him for a return to the game.

He made it back again in 2009, but never managed to regain his edge. Needless to say, his position as a leading attacker in the team became history. Eduardo left Arsenal after scoring only two goals in a total of eleven post injury games.

He later spent four years in Ukraine playing for Shakhtar Donetsk. He's now playing in Club do Flamengo in Brazil. Eduardo is just 32 years old.

Why am I mentioning this?

I'm using Eduardo story as actual proof of what can happen to any player who doesn't take care of his build.

Da Silva was a high quality player and could have become one of the best in the game. His mistake, and probably the Arsenal medical team's mistake as well, was not to work on his strength.

Soccer is a demanding game. That means the players have to be in good physical condition at all times. Fitness alone is not enough.

You need all the joints to be strong and protected with adequate muscle. For most players, this means it's necessary to spend time in the gym.

Accidents can, and sometimes do, happen to anyone. But having a strong physical body can protect you a lot.

Even if you get injured, the chances are the injury will be less severe if you've got a bit of meat and muscle on your bones.

Furthermore, the recovery time will be less too, in most cases at least. A star player owes it to himself, his team, and his fans to take good care of protecting himself against hurt and injury.

Eduardo injury took a couple of years from his career, but that's not all. It also made him afraid, or more cautious, on his return to the game.

He never got back to using his full potential to challenge defenders and attack the ball, not like he used to. A strikers' performance declines faster than defenders and goalkeepers anyway.

So losing so much time to a single injury was a devastating blow for Eduardo. On his return, it was relatively easy for most defenders to steal a ball from him.

It never used to be like that. It was also easy to win a physical challenge against him. Why? It was because Eduardo had become nervous about getting hurt again, afraid of a repeat injury.

Vassiriki Abu Diaby

Former French player, Abou Diaby, was all set to become the next Patrcik Viera (former Manchester City Midfielder). In fact, he was on track to be one of the best defensive midfielders in the history of soccer.

Unfortunately, he wasn't strong enough to handle the beating that comes with this position. In total, he suffered 28 injuries in different parts of his body.

Because of this, he only got to play two games in the last three seasons. He now has no club to play for after his contract expired with Arsenal.

Diaby wasted a magnificent career. He lost out all because he didn't support his talent with enough physical strength.

If only he had worked on this area he could have had a long and glowing career in soccer.

A Solid Body Allows You to Take on Different Roles

No matter what, you can't allow yourself to become a seasonal player if you want to be one of soccer's best defenders. Seasonal players don't make it to be great players. Weak legs and muscles won't help you.

Four Rules to Increase Muscles

Make sure to spike up your protein intake

You might be aware that running, and other physical activities, breaks down muscle tissue. What you might not know is that a professional soccer player can run from between 8-10 km on average, per game.

This is something that can become a problem if the player doesn't get proper nutrition. In a worst case scenario, too much exertion and too little protein in the diet can put him into a state of catabolism. This occurs when the body starts to break down muscle tissue.

It does this to provide energy to supply the body's efforts when there is no other source to fall back on. The body's primary source of energy is from carbohydrates; its secondary source is fat.

The body's final, last resort energy source comes from muscle tissue. Note that using muscle tissue for energy is not a normal condition or a healthy one.

Your body will only start to use muscle tissue for energy under extreme conditions. In the case of a soccer player, this will occur when he's not consuming enough calories over an extended period.

So when a diet lacks nutritional value in some way, the body is unable to function as it should do under extreme conditions.

The best way to avoid catabolism is to keep your body fueled with balanced amounts of protein. The way to know whether you're getting enough protein is with a simple calculation. You have to include at least 1.5 grams of protein per day for each one pound of your body weight.

Protein is necessary as it helps to create amino acids inside your body. Without getting too technical, amino acids are responsible for the muscle building process.

They do this by repairing any damaged muscle fibers. This in turn, stops the breakdown and deterioration of muscle tissue.

When lifting, increase weights and decrease the range of your repetitions.

When adding muscle to your body, the goal is to increase your strength rather than your size. Yes, you have to build muscles to support your body against fractures and injuries. But no, you mustn't get too big. The important thing to be mindful of here is balance.

Too much muscle will slow you down and create a negative effect on your movements. Believe me, this is not something you want to happen when you're out there on the field.

Focus on becoming lean instead of exercising like a bodybuilder.

In this case you will be use maximal strength exercises. This is to build just enough muscle for extra strength and added protection. The idea here is to have the right amount of muscle to help maintain consistent performance.

You will have to lift heavy weights but only for a small number or repetitions. This will be something like 3-6 sets per exercise and from 1-5 reps per set. You need to also take adequate rests to recover between sets. It's important to only perform a small number of exercises for each training session. Remember, you are not to exercise like a bodybuilder.

Multi–joint exercises are the way to go.

You don't want to focus on isolation exercises.

That type of exercise places an emphasis on a single muscle or muscle group. It's better for you to work on multi–joint exercises. This way you get to incorporate more muscles in a single exercise.

These will include exercises like squats, dead lifts, and bench presses. Others are clean and jerk, lunges and shoulder presses. Make a note of these as they are the ones you need to focus on in your training sessions.

36. Not Being Aware of the Other Team's Attempts to Waste More Time

This is something that happens a lot in soccer. It occurs most when one team is leading in the score and there's not long to go before the end of the game.

The winning team wants to hold on to their lead and reduce the time the losing side has to score. So they decide that wasting time is the best way to disrupt the game and hold on to their lead.

One of the most common ways to time-waste is to fake an injury. In this situation a player falls to the ground, often exaggerating his hurt.

He exaggerates to draw attention to himself. He may roll around in seeming agony, almost as if someone has shot him with a gun.

Others might fall on their own, complaining of cramps or pulled muscles. These are quite typical time-wasting tactics.

The use of substitutions is another way to delay a game. Kick-ins and throw-ins are two more. In these cases the player might take their time retrieving the ball, and even longer to put it back in play.

To stop the opposing team from wasting your time, try to avoid kicking the ball out. You must also never stop the play anytime one of your opponents fakes an injury. This is especially important when you're certain it's a put on.

My advice is to keep playing while the opponent is on the ground. This way, and providing the ref doesn't blow his whistle, you can use his trick to your advantage.

If you don't stop, and the ref doesn't blow his whistle, you have one less player to worry about at that moment.

I've already covered why you must never stop play unless you hear the referee's whistle. You can find that in chapter 28, "Not Playing on the Referee's Whistle."

37. Not Fighting for Every Ball

To be great you must die for every single ball. You must expect to either get the ball or clear it away with every attempt.

You need to win every ball that comes into your area, or at least expect to. Anyone who tells you different is either lying or has another agenda.

The greatest defenders in the world of soccer are the ones who treat all balls equal. Fast or slow, near or far, they look at each ball as a serious threat on their goal and to their team. Even when it's not, the passion and determination is the same as if it were.

Before you jump to the next paragraph, ask yourself who the best defenders in the world are right now? See if you can guess who the highest paid defenders are in European soccer, and ask yourself why that is.

OK, to save time here's the answer: Silva, Diego Godin, David Luis and Sergio Ramos. I will take Diego Godin as an example.

The Uruguayan defender plays for Atletico Madrid. Many soccer fans consider Godin to be one of the best five defenders in the world. He's also one of the best defenders and team leaders in the history of the Uruguay team.

I believe the main reason behind Godin's huge success is his fighting spirit. You can witness his sheer determination on every single ball and every single play.

Watch him and you will know. See how he's super tenacious with every ball, every tackle and every header. He's like this for the duration of the entire game.

These are the qualities that have seen him captain both Uruguay and Atletico Madrid at such a young age. He's 29 now, and has been the captain for both teams since he was 25 years old.

Why is this, really? It's because he is aggressive and he's willing to do whatever it takes to keep his goal area clean.

It is as simple as that, and he's always consistent in his style. He has leadership skills and an unwavering determination to triumph.

His approach to soccer is not so much a skill as a mental state. His mindset is a positive one, always hungry for success. This is how he maintains his unrelenting determination. He expects nothing but victory, and he often gets what he wants.

The good thing about having the right mental state is that you can acquire it if you don't have it. All you have to do is make a decision to change your thought process and your thoughts will then change. OK, so it's a little more complicated than that, but not by much.

Not every player is born a fighter, but that doesn't mean they can't become one. Never settle for what you are if it's not what you want to be.

If you are serious about making a shift in your attitude, then you can do it. A quote from the late self-help author and motivational speaker, Dr. Wayne Dyer, sums this up beautifully:

"If you change the way you look at things, the things you look at change."

38. Not Being Familiar with Attacker's Tricks

In this chapter we take a look at some of the attacker's tricks to look out for. Once you are familiar with these, you will be in a much better position to defend.

Running Diagonally to Beat the Offside

Here's a common trick that you need to be aware of.

Oftentimes, an attacker will try to beat the offside trap or escape from defenders to receive a through pass.

In these situations he will most likely run in a diagonal or sideways direction rather than straight toward the goal.

The reason they run in a diagonal direction instead of a vertical one is so that they can escape the defense in a safe way. It means they get to reach the ball without falling for the offside trap.

It's too easy to fall in the offside when running vertically, toward the goal. This is because a vertical run makes you more aware of their moves and direction.

This would allow you to act quick and put the attacker in the offside. When he runs in a diagonal direction, you're both away from the last rival defender and still on side.

Escaping Isolation by Moving to the Middle

In general, attackers depend on speed as the best way to get rid of defenders or to escape from them.

Their speed is their best weapon in these situations.

They will also take off whenever they find themselves isolated.

They will most certainly run off when they have no chance to receive the ball from their play makers. So they need to move fast, especially when their side becomes outnumbered.

In cases where the attacker finds himself out of the game, he has no choice but to go and look for the ball himself.

What he will likely do is head to the middle of the field so that he can receive early passes from his midfielders. When this happens, avoid chasing after him.

Leave that to your defensive midfielders. Going after him will not only exhaust you but it will also leave a gap in your defensive line.

Instead, let him exhaust himself since he will now have to cover a wider area of the field. Play smart and wait for him to come to you in these situations.

Making Intelligent Runs off the Ball to Disrupt Opponent's Defense and Formation

A smart attacker may try to offer help to the other attacker playing next to him. He does this by making smart, well–timed runs.

His hope is that the rival defenders will follow him, thus taking pressure away from his teammate. If you see this happen, the way you respond depends on how well you have read to the situation.

If he runs away from the area, toward the midfield (as in the previous example), you need to stay put. There is an exception to this decision though.

If you believe his move will create immediate danger for your team, then it is best to go after him. In this case, you will want another teammate to take your position so that you don't leave a gap in your defense.

The only safe way to do this is if it's part of your game plan. In other words, you and your team have discussed what to do if a situation like this occurs.

You do this before the game begins. There certainly won't be any time to discuss things once the game is on and that ball is rolling.

39. Not Knowing How to Play in Different Weather Conditions

Every weather condition carries its own set of difficulties for defenders. That means you must be well-prepared to play in all kinds of weather and under all circumstances. We will now take a look at each of these in turn, staring with wet and rainy conditions.

Playing on Wet or Rainy Days

Playing soccer on wet and rainy days means the ball is going to be heavier. This requires the defender exerts extra power when he strikes the ball. Beside the weight of the ball, another setback of playing in the rain is that it can affect vision.

This is a particular problem when trying to intercept crosses and high balls. There are problems for goalkeepers too. A wet and or muddy ball is so much more difficult to catch and control than a dry ball.

Wet and rainy days pose problems for all team players and not only defenders and goalkeepers. Those who lack experience, or are just not educated on how to play in the wet, will fare the worse.

As a defender you need to keep a strong focus on the ball at all times. You must always remember to provide extra coverage for your keeper too, if you play as a center back.

Make sure you've got his back anytime he leaves the box to clear a cross away. Note that in wet conditions, your keeper will most likely use his fist to punch the ball.

He will do this because trying to catch a wet ball can often be too risky. It's even riskier if it's covered in mud as well.

No one likes to play soccer when it's raining or when the field is soaking wet. But the reality is that games do still go on in these conditions.

For this reason, it's important that you practice and prepare for competing on wet and rainy days.

221

Playing on Windy Days

When the wind blows the ball will move faster in one direction and slower in another. The ball will also change its direction, either a little or a lot. It all depends on the strength of the wind and whether there are any cross winds or not.

The best way for a defender to deal with windy conditions is to never wait for a cross. If you do wait, then any sudden deflection in the ball's direction will most likely result in you losing it.

It's better to run toward the ball and meet it at the time and point you believe is right. You are then in a better position to head the ball and send it to where you need it to go.

Most teams prefer to rely on crosses and high balls in windy conditions. The team that plays against the wind is always at a disadvantage.

The team with the wind behind them usually gets to benefit from the mistakes the other side makes. It's harder for them to receive a ball or clear it away, no thanks to the unpredictable nature of wind. That's bad news for them but great news for you.

Both sides will have to play with the wind against them for half the game. The better you can play with the wind against you, the better your chances are of winning.

If you can anticipate the unpredictable nature of wind, you will have more success on the field. Of course, when the wind is on your side things are much easier and less strenuous.

You get to send crosses and long through-balls with additional speed and more precision. When the wind is on your side, and you know how to use it to best effect, you get to create some serious scoring opportunities.

But you need your skills and extra efforts most when the wind is against you, so make sure you prepare for that.

Be ready for balls that deflect back from the goalkeeper. He won't have the luxury of catching some of the shots if there's a strong wind.

This is an even bigger problem for him on days that are gusty. Strong gusts create all kinds of problems for every player, but the goalie has the hardest time of all.

The most frustrating thing for him is the sudden change in ball direction as he attempts to save shots at his goal.

Playing on Sunny Days

Sunny days might sound perfect but they too can have their own problems. In general though, a defender should be able to make a great performance when it's dry and bright. That's providing there are no strong winds disrupting play of course.

On days where the sun is high in the sky, the vision will be clear and the movement easy. But there is still something that a defender should prepare for when he plays in sunny conditions.

That is his inability to see the ball properly whenever the sun blocks his vision.

This will depend on where the ball's coming from in relation to where he's receiving it. The defender must also be extra vigilant if his keeper has the sun in his eyes.

When the sun is low in the sky, it can cause huge problems for all players on the side playing with the sun in front of them.

So there will be times when it's hard to see the approaching ball because the sun is low and in your eyes.

In these situations you have to reply more on instinct and experience. What I mean by this is that you will have to predict the ball's speed and direction.

Of course, the accuracy of your prediction is something that comes better with experience. But you have no choice but to guess, whether you're experienced or not.

During the 2002 FIFA World Cup in South Korea and Japan, a Turkish goalkeeper had a unique approach for dealing with the sun. It was a strange, yet effective method, at least for the Turkish goalkeeper, Rustu Reçber.

He would paint the skin below his eyes with a black ink, or something similar. He did this so that neither the light of the sun nor the stadium's strong spot lights would distract him or affect his vision too much.

He played just great in that tournament too. In fact, he could have won the Golden Glove Award for his outstanding performance.

It was the German legend, Oliver Kahn, who prevented Reçber getting the Golden Glove. It was unlucky for Reçber that Kahn gave the performance of his life in that competition. Because of that he got to snatch this prestigious award for himself.

Juve's legend, Edgar Davids, actually used to wear sunglasses when he played. The Surinamese-born Dutch midfielder did this to protect his eyes. His right eye needed special protection after surgery to treat a condition known as glaucoma.

Davids later revealed that wearing glasses on the field helped him to perform better in different weather conditions. He said that his glasses were especially useful on sunny days. Some players would be distracted playing in sunglasses, but it worked for Davids, and that's all that mattered to him.

Whatever approach you take to help your performance in various weather conditions is fine. That's as long as it works for you and doesn't break any of soccer's rules, of course.

40. Not Meditating Before Games

Many soccer players attribute their calmness and high state of focus to meditation. Yes, these big tough guys have daily meditation and mindfulness routines.

Some players claim to meditate not just once but twice on their game nights. This is even more likely whenever they have a big important game the following day.

The former Dutch forward, Dennis Bergkamp, and former Danish goalkeeper, Peter Schmeichel, swore by the benefits of meditation.

Science has shown that meditation has many positive benefits. To begin with, it boosts self-confidence, self-esteem and general wellbeing. It also increases optimism and self-awareness.

Some ADHD sufferers have also found advantages in meditation. For thousands of years those who meditate swear by the benefits of this ancient practice.

But it has only been in more recent times that The West has embraced this old practice from The East.

As a defender, meditation will help to enhance your ability to make critical decisions. It will also help you to manage distractions and put you in better control more generally.

Let's look at some of these benefits in a bit more detail.

Meditation Helps You to Keep Your Eyes on the Ball

Monitoring the "ball" and keeping the "ball" away from danger is a defender's main responsibility. You may wonder why I highlighted the word "ball" twice. I did this to emphasize how important the "ball" is. Too many defenders lose focus and sight of the ball at just the wrong moment.

This is something that can, and often does, cost their team dearly. Just a momentary loss of focus on the ball can have dire consequences.

It often results in what would otherwise have been easily intercepted balls getting lost. What happens is that the defender places his focus on the man he's marking, or his leg movements.

That might sound logical, but it's not. His focus should always be on the ball, not on the man. Anything other than the ball is low priority. I will illustrate this point using the fly swatting analogy.

OK, so have you ever tried to kill a fly with a fly swatter? If yes, then you will know just how difficult this can be.

In fact, if you don't keep your eyes fixed on the fly, swatting it becomes an impossible task. Well, the same thing happens when you're attempting to intercept a soccer ball during a game.

In this case the ball is the fly and you are trying to get it. Unless you keep your eyes fixed on it, meaning only the ball, your task is much less likely to succeed.

There are two ways to enhance your focus so that you can keep your eyes fixed firmly on the ball at all times. To be any good at defending, you really do need to develop sticky eyes. Here's what those two methods are:

1. Video Games
2. Meditation

I would suggest you dedicate a suitable amount of your time to play air hockey. You can use a real table or play it as a video game. Air hockey is one of the best mental games for defenders and goalkeepers bar none.

Here's why: Air hockey improves a defender's responses and a goalkeeper's reflexes. It helps maintain those sticky eyes I was referring to. Air hockey is a lot of fun too, which makes it an enjoyable training session.

Get a friend to compete with, or if that's not doable play the video game version. If you opt for the video game, be sure to set it on an advanced mode as soon as you are able. I can guarantee you will develop sticky eyes using this method. That's providing you put in the time to practice of course.

We've already looked at the benefits of meditation. If it all sounds a bit too "spiritual" for you, and not really your thing, then try to view it in a different way. Look at meditation as nothing more than sitting still in a quiet space for a set period of time.

After all, that's what it is, in its most basic form at least. Set aside just 15-30 minutes a day for a week, and at the same time each day. You will know by the end of your seven day trial whether you want to carry on or not.

How to Meditate

- Wear something loose-fitting and comfortable.
- Find a calm space to practice.
- Switch off your mobile and any other distracting devices.
- Get into a comfortable sitting position with your feet resting flat on the floor.
- Close your eyes and focus on your breath, breathing in through your nose and out through the mouth.
- Stay put and stay still for the time you have set aside.

You will have all kinds of thoughts and distractions when you first start to meditate. This is quite normal, so don't think you're failing if you find it hard to still the mind at first. Let any thoughts come and go from your mind.

Don't try to control them or get into internal conversations. Just allow them to happen. Your aim here is to just watch your thoughts as an outside observer.

OK, so the above guide is the most basic level of meditation. If you feel you want to get deeper into this there is a plethora of great advice and information on the web.

41. Not Having Enough Motivation

Always keep in mind that nothing worth venturing ever comes easy. But that's a good thing because it makes us feel so much better when we achieve difficult tasks.

Success, in any area in life, not only in soccer, requires passion, ambition, patience, persistence, and a huge amount of hard work.

For every one great player you know of, or chant for, there will be thousands of others who failed to make the grade. These are the majority of hopefuls that get lost and forgotten.

Every player who made his name into your memory had that special something. But make no mistake about it, none of these guys got to where they are with ease.

Not even those who possess natural talent. Talent without work is indeed a useless attribute. Players with no natural talent can still make the big time.

They have to apply extra of everything to get there, but some do, despite the odds. They make it because they are passionate about playing soccer.

Their determination is unwavering and they never give up, not even if others tell them they have no chance of making it.

There are some who enjoy the game but it doesn't run through their blood like the determined types above. They are the guys who are attracted mainly by the money and the glamourous side of soccer.

These are the wrong reasons for wanting to be a big time soccer star. Because of that, those attracted to the game only because of the money will never make the grade.

The demand for talented players is a lot less than the supply. There will be tens of thousands of young players the world over who all aspire to reach the big time.

But there will only ever be a tiny handful of available slots in professional soccer to accommodate the few. So the competition is tough, to put it mildly.

Only the best of the best will stand a chance. Talent scouts look for passion and potential.

They can spot things in players that others can't see, even the players themselves. People are often surprised at how a lesser talented player is sometimes picked over the more talented one.

It's because the scout saw something in that player that set him apart. Never underestimate potential. Some good defenders might have reached their potential. Others might still have plenty of growth left in them. Talent scouts are good at spotting these things.

What It Takes to Be a Star Player

You will need a great amount of motivation. Your energy, effort and mental toughness should be relentless.

You must go through injuries, exercises and strict physical conditioning programs. You have to strive to be better than everyone else that you know.

Doing all this won't come easy. You need to be willing to go beyond pain, disappointment and failure.

You will encounter setbacks along the way, that's inevitable. But you cannot let setbacks deter your spirit or dampen your motivation.

Nobody can put your off trying, and if they do, you work even harder to prove your worth.

You will have your own reasons to fuel your fires of passion. Maybe you're determined to prove to yourself that you can succeed.

Or perhaps you are trying to prove your worth to all the naysayers who said you're living in a dream world. Where your determination and motivation comes from isn't important.

What's important is that your hunger for success is enough to keep you going. You push and never stop pushing, no matter what obstacles stand in your way. It's like the old song goes: "When the going gets tough the tough get going."

So before you start out on your mission, make sure you know what your core reason is for wanting to be one of soccer's greats. Once you find your reason(s), hold on to it/them like your life depends on it.

Leadership Is a Quality That Forces You to Have and Pass on Motivation

If you want to become a world class defender, then you have to understand that you must be a leader. In this sense, a leader must be able to motivate his team whatever the state of play might be.

You must also be a master of disguise. By that, I mean even if you don't happen to feel motivated yourself, you have to look and act as if you are.

Here are three great examples of defensive leaders: Patrick Vieira, Didier Deschamps and Carles Puyol. They have persistent motivation and do a good job at inspiring their other teammates. Vieira was the captain of Cannes at the age of just 19 years old.

Deschamps managed to keep his teammates inspired through tough competitions. He succeeded to lead players like Zidane, Henry and Robert Pires to win their first world cup title. He did all this despite the many problems the French team had before the beginning of the tournament.

I watched Deschamps play in the 1998 championship. You could see how juiced up his teammates got once they saw him intercept a ball or make a great header. He was impressive to say the least, despite his age and despite being short at just 1.74m.

He would motivate any teammate who messed up with a wrong pass or a wrong shot. He would do this by letting him know that it's okay, and that the team still needs him. The key here is to maintain momentum. If that's lost, so are motivation and a winning attitude. Deschamps is a pro at keeping momentum high.

To become the great defender you want to be, you too must show real leadership skills. Your job is to transfer confidence, faith and determination to all your teammates.

This is even more important when the going gets tough and you guys are behind in the score.

Nobody likes being around weak defenders, the ones who quit at the first sign of danger. Fighters are the guys who get to lead and inspire.

They get to do this not out of force, but out of the respect their fellow teammates have for them. You will find that all famous defenders (especially center backs) have a strong character.

They have a kind of aura around them that radiates positivity wherever they go. These guys couldn't throw the towel in even if they wanted to. It's simply not in their character. They have that winning mentality that I often refer to.

Of course there will be bad days, or even a bad run or a poor season. Other times your team will play so bad that you want to throttle the guys rather than encourage them. But you don't do it. You're better than that. You understand that soccer is a team sport.

That means sticking together through thick and thin, the good times and the not so good. Unlike other positions, you understand the importance of the wider team effort. For you, your ego, your name, your reputation and your own enjoyment is not important.

If the team's strategy is not working, you look for ways to fix it. When players are feeling down, you pick them up.

You are a defender, and that means you defend your guys to the hilt. You do this come rain, come shine, come hell or high water. You lead by example because you are a winner, and winners never quit.

In life (not just soccer) most people look for someone to take the lead and guide them. Most of us aren't natural leaders, but we can learn to become great leaders if we aspire to be.

A good leader helps to motivate those who are unable to motivate themselves. This is especially important when the chips are down.

Defenders who have such qualities are not only rare but also valuable in the marketplace. If you want to make a living out of soccer, as a defender, you know what you have to do, you know now what you have to become.

42. Not Being Able to Quickly Recover After Making a Serious Mistake in the Game

For a few defenders, it only takes one bad mistake for them to mentally lose their focus for the rest of the game. Some even ask for a substitute to take their place if they make a silly slip that leads to the rivals scoring a goal.

Let's face it, it can be hard to hold your nerve and remain confident when deep inside you feel that this is not your day.

And there are times when a mistake you make is so big that it looks as though your team might lose because of it. In such situations it's hard to stop thinking about stuff. One big blunder can affect the entire team too, not just you.

This is especially true if your bad mood and worsening play is obvious to those around you. And if you make more than one slip up, you can't help but feel like an unwanted presence on the field.

And the more your side is losing in the score, the more difficult it becomes for you to continue on. Some of you reading here will be able to relate to all of these things.

These situations are not that uncommon, but they needn't be as bigger deal or as intense as many make them out to be.

Most can relate to the above setbacks as young amateurs trying to progress in the game. But it is only those who use their mistakes to learn and develop from who get to shine above all others.

Here's something to think about. The words hard, difficult and impossible are the words of average people. They are excuse words used to justify incompetence or poor performance. The time you've spent so far reading this book, it's my guess that you have come to realize something.

That is, this book is NOT for average defenders or day dreamers. This book is for those who want big things. It is for doers not fantasists who never move past the "if only" stage. Those of you reading here will want to leave a mark in both soccer and defending history.

Leave the "excuse words" for the average players to excuse themselves with. For you, look at hard, difficult and impossible situations as challenges. Don't look at them as something to fear and run from.

Live in the Moment

You must build the habit of staying in the now. The power of NOW is incredible. It's never ever any other time. It's always NOW, and it always will be NOW.

Yet so many amateur players are anywhere but now in their thoughts. They drift between the past and the future. All too often they run "if-only this," or "what-if that," scenarios through their minds.

Learning from the past and preparing for what's ahead are things that have their place in soccer. But they have no place when you need to be in the here and now.

To maintain your peak performance after making a huge mistake you need to be present. That means you have to be in the now and deal with events as they are, at that precise moment in time.

To dwell on what's just happened is a recipe for failure. If your team is not performing well, and you're far behind in the score, the only way out is to perform better.

It means the team's performance has to change right now. Understand that you can't bring about any changes if your focus is anywhere but in the present moment.

So you must isolate your mind and not think about the past. You must also isolate your mind to stop you from visualizing a miserable future outcome. I know that a shift in mindset is easier to say than it is to do.

Even so, nobody ever said soccer was an easy game. In fact, if soccer was easy, then serious players wouldn't enjoy it. They would most likely opt to play something else instead.

OK, let us look at how to get that shift in attitude which is so crucial to the role of a defender. I will do this by first explaining something outside of soccer, so bear with me here.

Albert Einstein once said:

"You can't solve a problem with the same mentality that created the problem in the first place".

You might just want to read that over a few times to get the real gist of it. Also, look at your own game and see if there is any connection to Einstein's quote in the way you approach things.

Here's a non-soccer example to illustrate this mad approach.

Suppose a Trojan virus has somehow infected your computer. Because of this infection, your computer no longer works as it should do.

The first and most logical thing for you to do is to run a full virus scan in an attempt to get rid of the intrusion. This is a logical response to this particular problem.

Now let's say that the virus checker doesn't find the virus. Worse still is that it actually causes even more problems for you by removing critical files that your system needs to function. In this case, your problem has just gotten a lot worse by your attempts to fix it.

Someone with a negative mindset might try to fix the problem by running and rerunning a full system scan over and over. He does this even though the results are always the same, or worse, after each new attempt.

He's wasting his time, his energy, and his peace of mind with each new try. He becomes agitated and experiences enormous stress. All that's happening here is that he's getting nowhere real fast. Yet despite it all, he continues to rinse and repeat the same failed procedure.

Some might even say it's a form of madness to continue in this way. I would agree that such an approach does seem bonkers. Yet haven't we all been guilty of this behavior at some point in time?

Einstein also said:

"The definition of insanity is doing the same thing over and over and expecting different results."

The difference between a successful personality and an unsuccessful one is the thoughts we feed into the mind. False beliefs and negative thinking are what bug a pessimistic mindset. If you can relate, then don't despair. This doesn't mean you're doomed to a life of misery and failure on the field. That's providing you are open for positive change.

The only way for a negative mind to reach successful conclusions is to move things around a bit. You do this by getting rid of old negative thinking patterns.

You then exchange them for new, more positive thoughts and beliefs. Sometimes it might be necessary to fake things till you get to make it.

This is perfectly okay if that's the approach you need. You see, for any pattern or bad habit to change for the better, replacing it with something else is the only way.

You can't just stop believing a certain way and hope that's enough, because it just won't work.

The best way to transform your life is to find a good mentor, dead or living. This needs to be someone who thinks and believes how you would like to think and believe. "*Out with the old, and in with the new*," as the saying goes. So once you find someone who succeeds in a way that you would also like to flourish, then you need to tell yourself this:

From now on, this is exactly how I will think and act to achieve my own goals.

What you are doing here is borrowing the mindset of someone else, just until you get to develop your own. You are not trying to become a clone of another person. You are just applying their thought patterns and approach to life, and planting them into your own psyche.

From here, these new, borrowed thought patterns will shape over time to work with your own unique character.

So are you ready to ditch your old mindset completely? If it hasn't helped you to succeed so far, then I think you know the answer to that.

Duplicating another person's mindset is a proven technique. It has been successful for many players who have adopted it.

You don't have to have a mentor if you would sooner not. I think the mentor approach is the best one, but you can still do this alone if you prefer.

All you have to do is just recognize your own negative thinking patterns. Once you know what they are, you can then get to work at swapping the negative with the positive.

You're probably keen to start working on this right away. Your question now will be this: How can I maintain mental toughness and stay emotionally strong when the game is not going too well?

Well, as you know, it all has to start with a shift in how you think. If you haven't found the mindset of a mentor to borrow, you can start to develop your own from scratch. Here are two simple rules that you need to be mindful of. These will lay the foundation for you:

1. Understand that blaming yourself and thinking about the past always hurts you, it can never help you. So STOP blaming yourself

2. Remind yourself that successful defenders neglect the past on the field. They are always in the present, thinking about what to do NOW so that they can succeed with their next move.

It is only when you change the way you look at things that the things you look at can change. Mindset is something that needs developing, just like any other skill.

It's a good idea to set a couple of hours aside in the day to listen to audio books about success and successful people. You can include the 10 X Rule in this, in fact I recommend it.

I used to do this early in the morning, before I began my day, and again in the evening, usually just before bed time.

When you sandwich your days like this, with positive feedback, it helps to build a whole new mentality. This is not only going to help you on the field, but in everyday living too.

When you start to think and act how successful people do, then you will become more successful in you endeavors.

Work at these things and you will become amazed at just how quick you get to recover on the field from bad situations. There will still be those times when you or your team makes a major mistake or falls behind in the score.

But the way you react, or not, as the case may be, will be so much different. Strive to be successful and you will succeed.

43. You Are Afraid of Getting Hit or Getting Injured

In many situations, a defender will fear going after a ball or making a certain move or a tackle. His reason will be that he's afraid of getting hurt or suffering a serious injury.

The saddest thing about this problem is that it's so unnecessary. At least in most cases it is. Many of these guys have the physical capability to be great defenders.

They also have the necessary skills to succeed. What's lacking, though much needed, is the courage to go into situations that are difficult.

Such a situation might mean a full-on physical challenge with someone bigger and tougher. But a defender's job is to defend, and that means against anyone and everyone, and in all situations.

What these guys need is a strong boost of determination and courage. Some will develop it whereas most others won't. It doesn't take much to guess who will go on to succeed and who will remain as just another Average Joe defender.

There is nothing wrong or weak about being afraid. No one in their right mind relishes the thought of getting hurt or injured. It makes perfect sense to protect ourselves from these things.

This is what we call healthy fear. All living creatures, and that includes humans, are programmed to avoid pain and suffering.

Without a healthy fear, we simply could not survive and thrive as a species. But there's healthy fear and unhealthy fear, and here lies the difference. In other words, fear has its place but it needs to be healthy, and kept in perspective.

When it comes to the role of defender, any unhealthy fear brings with it caution. And with caution comes hesitancy. Any defender who hesitates will underperform.

It's important to know the facts about fear. This way you get to understand the difference between justified and unjustified fears. As you do this you also get to learn which fears are overblown when it comes to soccer.

Once you have fear put into some sort of perspective, your mindset should change for the better. Your goal here is to have less fear and more bravery in all areas of your game.

Bravery will see you take more action and improve the outcome of your defending. It will make you more successful than fear and caution ever could.

And the braver you are, the more confident you become in your ability to defend. A great defender is tough in both the physical and the mental sense.

If you already play as a defender, then you are already brave to some extent.

The question you need to ask yourself is am I brave enough, could I be any braver? Developing bravery is more to do with psychology than physical ability.

As a defender (especially a center back or stopper) you cannot allow fear to occupy too much of your mind.

Learn how to tell the difference between healthy (justified), and unhealthy (unjustified) fears. Once you can do this, you get to limit fear to a specific set of situations and conditions on the field.

Many people nowadays have evolved into namby-pambies. By that, I mean they are afraid of just about everything, including their own shadows. They have become so fearful that it prevents them from living life to the full. To play as a defender is to play a tough game.

You are, to all intents and purposes, a warrior on the field. There is no place for over-caution, or unjustifiable fears in your role.

A lot of defensive players will develop a particular fear for a certain type of play. It might be because the last time they got involved they suffered hurt or injury. Or maybe they know of, or saw a situation that triggered fear inside their minds.

Let's take Mikel Arteta as an example. Arteta plays as a defensive midfielder for Arsenal. He has suffered many injuries since he joined the club in 2011.

With each new injury he lost a bit more of his fire. Over time, he started to become less aggressive when playing in the middle. This resulted in him losing too many easy balls.

He became too cautious because he got too fearful. He worried about getting hurt or sustaining yet another injury. When things like this happen to a player their value becomes less.

In Arteta's case, his lack of aggressive play saw him lose his position as the team's number one stopper. The job went to his teammate, Francis Coquelin. Worth noting here is that his French counterpart is 10 years younger than him.

Some center backs become afraid of a hit to the head or breaking their nose. You can see this in the way that a lot of amateurs play.

They develop the habit of closing their eyes when going in hard. You can often see them reach for a header half-heartedly lest they get injured.

To get rid of this fear you have to put things into some kind of perspective. Just ask yourself how many serious injuries are there with defenders in the majority of games. When you do this you get to realize that the probability of getting hurt or injured is quite low.

Because of that you have to ask yourself if it's worth losing the ball or conceding a goal all because there's a slight chance you could get hurt. There will be even less chance of you getting injured.

Why You Feel Afraid

You feel afraid because you think too much. That's it, in a nutshell.

Let me put it another way. Fear on the soccer field is not real. It is a product of the thoughts you create inside your own mind.

Danger is real, but fear is a choice. It's important to distinguish between the two things. Defending is all about courage, determination and tenacity.

And the best way to kill all these things off is by thinking too much about what might happen. Stinking thinking can only result in self-doubt. And any doubts about your ability to succeed in a given situation will results in failure.

When you think too much about the wrong stuff and not enough about the right actions, there will always be negative consequences.

It will destroy both the quality and quantity of your actions. This applies not only to soccer but in all areas of life.

How to Deal with Over-Thinking

When you're out there on the field, in any situation, stop thinking and start doing. To put it another way, let your instincts take over.

If you've been playing for a while, you should intuitively know how to deal with most of the common plays. As you already know, soccer is about timing and fast actions.

Over-thinking and fear are two peas of the same pod. Both of these things will see a dramatic delay in your timing, and you know what the consequence of that is.

Consider F.E.A.R as False Evidence Appearing Real. This is exactly what it is in most situations on the field. Keep moving and take action right away, refuse to let fear dare to interfere with your game.

Move closer to the striker, spread your legs and open your eyes. Be willing to do whatever it takes to clear that ball away from your penalty area.

Many defensive players spend years playing without a single injury. Are they just lucky? Well, it's possible that luck plays some part. But it's my guess they avoid injury because they're fast acting and confident.

Those who are slow to act and overcautious bring a lot of problems on themselves. Being hesitant makes them more prone, not less prone, to accidents and injuries.

It's a bit like the slow and overly cautious drivers on the roads. They think they are safer, yet they are more prone to having an accident, or causing one, than other drivers. The drivers who moves forward with confidence and make quick decisions are the safest of all.

I will end this chapter with a couple of powerful quotes:

"We die if we worry and we die if we don't. So why worry?"

You see, worrying about suffering a rare injury hinders your progress. Wrapping yourself up in cotton wool takes the fun out of defending. And without the "fun" element, there's no point. Be mindful of the fact that thinking will never overcome fear, but action will.

"The only thing we have to fear is fear itself." ~ *Franklin D. Roosevelt*

44. Not Learning from the Pros

To learn requires action. We do learn some things at the subconscious level, of course. But to learn something new, and to good effect, you must make a conscious decision to study and then act.

The capacity to learn is a gift that we should all embrace. The ability to learn something well is a skill. The willingness to learn is a choice, and one that all great defenders choose to do.

I have found that learning about soccer always teaches me something new. There is no graduation here, but there is potential to reach great heights. At least there is for those who embrace learning and never stop.

Watch videos, and watch them often. Because you're reading this book, it's my guess you are already obsessed with the game. You are here because you want to enhance your ball skills.

But you can only learn so much by reading a book. Other medium like TV, videos, and live games should all be a part of your learning routine.

Don't just watch the soccer superstars play, STUDY them. Try to mimic their style. Look for things that you might not have otherwise thought about doing.

Discover flaws in your own style from the mistakes that you make. Embrace failures and setbacks as great learning tools.

Don't underestimate online video. This is a medium that wasn't around just 10-15 years ago. You should welcome this free format as much as you can. Save clips of plays and players who inspire you.

Watch, re-watch, pause and replay till your heart's content. Both the quality and the quantity of what you can learn from watching and duplicating from video is vast.

Start to build a healthy obsession for the defender position. Don't let anyone or anything convince you that you're not good enough.

You need to take your game to the next level and make it a real passion. There's no such thing as a part time soccer great.

If you want to realize your dreams you have to live and breathe those dreams. So take action, and never stop learning. At the end of every day, set yourself a challenge.

Make a promise to know of something, or know how to do something new, that you didn't know about the day before. It might be something major or minor, that's not the point.

The point is to just learn. Learning is a mode that you can get into. The more you learn about the things you love, the more you want to know.

Caution! The opposite is also true. By not learning something new on a regular basis is a trap. It often results in procrastination.

It doesn't mean you don't want to learn new things, it just means you can't be bothered right now. It's a trap you want to avoid at all costs. And the way to avoid it is by learning some fact, or some new skill, every single day, big or small.

Understand what I am about to say: You don't have too much time to waste if you're to flourish at an early age. You might be young now, but the retirement age for most professional soccer players is also young.

The sooner you get into the winning mindset, the sooner important people get to notice you. This is not a career that you might want to look into when you're in your mid-twenties.

Before you reach the age of 18 or 20, most of your soccer skills and attributes should be well-developed. I would say to about 60-70% percent of their full potential.

There is always room for improvement at any age and level in soccer, or course. But you won't be able to start from the bottom up if you're already in your 20s.

So yes, there is plenty of room for playing great soccer at any age. The passion doesn't have to die out just because a player is older. But if you want to reach the professional level, playing for the big teams, then this really is a young man's game.

Don't try to reinvent the wheel. You don't have time to look into new and fancy ways to play. Your own unique style will develop as you train, so just let it happen. All you need to do is stick with the basics here.

There will be plenty of time to add your own little touches later on. For now though, learn from the greats, and never stop learning.

It has been my experience that the best things in life materialize by taking fast actions. Thinking too much is nothing but a hindrance.

In fact, it can stall your efforts or even put you off trying. The only way to succeed at anything is by doing. This approach has never failed me and the results have always been greater than I could have imagined.

One of the most important lessons you can learn is this: you will only get out of something what you put into it. Put in the time, the effort, and the commitment, and great things will come to pass.

Take it from me, the best and fastest way to learn anything you watch online is to work on what you see.

That means right away, the second you have a minute. So that's not in a few days or when you have the next practice session, but right away. I assume you have a soccer ball and an area to practice in, so get to practice.

Remember the power of NOW that we talked about in a previous chapter? Well, that applies to learning too. Excuses have no place in the world of a wannabe soccer superstars, so make sure you don't go looking for them.

This get-up-and-go approach is what will help you to stand out from the pack. When you're into the action side of learning, don't forget the power of repetition.

Repeat the same play over and over until you get good at it. Once you can check a new skill off as "learned," switch over to a new one.

Don't delay because now you are in full leaning mode. It means your mind is tuned-in to learning; you are at your very best. You are in a position where you get to learn faster and with better results.

Don't break your momentum now that you have it. This is the approach and mindset of high achievers.

Use Cameras as a Learning Tool

Recording your performance using video is invaluable to you. Footage like this can reveal a lot about the way you play. Video can highlight things to you about your game that you might not have otherwise noticed.

You can use video to identify your strengths and detect any weaknesses you might have. It is only when you get to identify flaws in your game that you can get to work at fixing them. Video can help a lot with this.

Thinking about stuff after an event and having things explained by others is also useful. Even so, the more tools you have at your disposal the better you will fare. It is only when you see yourself in pictures (moving and still) that you get to appreciate the power of the lens.

Your aim with video is to find out all there is to know about yourself and the way you perform on the field. If you want to see your playing style for what it is, then my suggestion is to use cameras, and use them a lot. You won't regret it.

Today you have a real advantage over the players of yesteryear. This is because most of you have Smartphones, Tablets or Phablets at your disposal. All these devices have inbuilt digital video functions, which makes recording both cheap and easy.

There is something important that you should acknowledge. It is the fact that even if you're a good player right now, exceptional even, you still have more to give.

No player should ever concede to the notion that he's about as good as he's likely to get. This just isn't true. There is always room for more.

Give me recorded footage of any amateur player and I can tell you all kinds of things about the individual. It won't take me long to spot the good and not so good areas of his playing style either.

More than 95 percent of the time I am right in my assessments. This is not because I have any kind of magic skill for spotting these things. It's simply because I have learned how to observe a player's performance as opposed to watching it.

All you need to know is that something can show up on film that is not always obvious by other methods of observation.

From video you get to identify bad footwork, distractions, any lapse in reading the game, and so on. It all comes out on film, once you know what to look for.

I recommend you ask a friend, or anyone who has good knowledge of soccer, to record you performance. It's also better if they know how to use a camera to best effect.

The first few attempts to record you in action might be a bit hit-and-miss, but that's okay. Just keep at it and you will soon have some fabulous footage taken from the best shooting angles.

You will always get some great advice and tips from your coach and other players. But there is nothing quite as valuable as seeing yourself on video.

If you want to fix, fine-tune, and add new skills to your toolkit, then start to record your performances.

Discuss Your Footage with the Coach

Once you have your video footage, you will want to share it with someone qualified to look at it objectively.

You can start by discussing your findings with your coach. Don`t end the discussion without setting a fixed plan. Between the two of you, decide what the next steps should be. You need to come up with a plan that helps you to overcome your weaknesses and/or gets rid of any mistakes.

The French goalkeeping coach, Christophe Lollichon, joined Chelsea in 2007. During his time at the English club, Lollichon has coached some great goalies. Petr Cech`s and Thaibut Courtois are two of the most famous. In an interview for Chelsea TV, Lollichon talked about what it's been like to work with two of the world's best goalkeepers.

Lollichon is a well-known coach and well-respected in the game too. So much so, that Petr Cech said something this summer that no one expected to hear.

He said that he won't sign up for Arsenal unless the club brings along his favorite coach as well.

That's quite some respect a goalkeeper has for his coach. Cech knows that he wouldn't have got to where he is today without the guidance of Lollichon. So why is that, what makes Lollichon so special? Well, maybe it's what he said in the interview that explains it the best.

Lollichon said that he and his staff use at least two cameras when they coach. They do this to track every single move that any of the keepers make on the field. Lollichon also said that he spends from 2-3 hours going over the most recent footage with his goalies.

They look at what he has done wrong and what he has done right. In other words, he doesn't just tell him to fix this or improve on that. He sits down and takes quality time with his keepers, reviewing the footage in great detail.

Only when everything is fully understood, do they then work on a plan together. They look at how best to fix any flaws and improve any existing strengths before the next game.

Compare Your Mistakes

Look at your mistakes objectively. This includes all the goals your team concedes, and the balls you fail to clear away. Compare your video footage with famous defensive players.

Use YouTube and other video sharing websites to find the clips. Cover your problem from all angles. Ask yourself what the professionals might have done, or did do, in the same or similar situations.

Compare your tackles with other defender's tackles, as well as your headers. Also look at your take-offs and the decisions you made at the time.

Look at your foot work as well, and your positioning in general. In short, you need to cover everything about your game. Leave no stone unturned as you scrutinize the video.

For you to record yourself, and then watch yourself play, is the best and most effective tool you have to learn about mistakes. It's also the fastest as you get to see things that might have otherwise gone unnoticed.

Many younger and older defenders alike will often repeat the same mistakes over and over. These are sometime quite subtle and hard to spot under usual conditions.

This is why video is so invaluable. Don't forget, you should have the option to play footage back in slow motions too. You will definitely be able to pause, stop, rewind, and replay. These are obviously not things we can do in real-world situations.

We looked earlier at how studying soccer's great defenders on video can be a great leaning method. Well, what you are doing now is learning from the exact same medium.

The first difference is that you're learning more about what not to do than what to do. And the second difference is that you're learning from yourself instead of others.

Today, video is cheap, it's effective, and it's portable, so make sure you use it. You'll be glad you did.

Final Thoughts

In this book, I have shown you everything you need to know about how to become a great defender. We have looked at how soccer's greats managed to build a reputation for themselves.

OK, it's now time for a final word. My last piece of advice to you is simple. In fact, it is so simple and short that I can sum it up in a single phrase: Take Action!

This is so obvious yet the one thing that many fail to do. It's true, there is so much lost talent out there. This is not because the individuals were at the wrong place at the wrong time either.

It's because they failed to take action. Whenever we don't follow through on our commitments, we can't expect much to come of our dreams.

Does this ring any bells with you? If yes, then you need to come up with a better plan. Failure to act will result in the situation remaining the same. To sum that up with a quote:

"If you always do what you've always done, then you'll always get what you've always got."

Your hopes and dreams of becoming a great defender will always stay as hopes and dreams if you fail to act.

Yes, it's sometimes painful to take action. And yes, it can be inconvenient at times, messing with other plans you might have. It can be demanding too, painful even.

But nothing is quite as disappointing as looking back on your life when you're older and having regrets.

You can see it all the time, as older guys ask themselves that age old question:

"I wonder what would have happened if only I had..."

It's important for you to acknowledge one very important fact. It is this: Every single LW, RW, CM, DM or AM you know the name of, even the most mediocre of them, has taken a great amount of action to get to where he's at.

So here's the deal with this book. Promise yourself that you will take positive, regular action based on what you now know. Aim to do this at least 10 times more than everybody else you know. Stick with the plan no matter what.

Create check lists if that helps. I'm serious. A bit of box-ticking can be a great motivational approach as you work through your action plan.

I hope that this book has inspired you. We have covered a lot and used many real-world examples to illustrate certain points. We've looked at what to do and what not to do. We have studied numerous tools and techniques.

These are the things that soccer's greats have used to help them excel in their careers. Yet despite all this, none of it is of any use unless you now put what you know into practice.

So again, my last word to you is to take positive action and follow your dreams. Don't give up just because someone tells you you're not good enough.

In fact, that is even more reason to press on than ever. Keep believing until you realize your dreams. Embed this quote into the forefront of your mind:

"The only real failure in life is the failure to try."

So remember to always, always, always believe in yourself. Do this even when stuff doesn't seem to be going according to plan. Actually, do this especially when things don't seem to be going according to plan.

Understand that you can't have progress without some setbacks along the way. In fact, failures and setbacks are instrumental in the learning progress. Try to look at any failures as something which helps, not hinders, your progress.

Be mindful of this whenever things start to get tough. You must believe in yourself. If you don't, then those who you need for encouragement and support won't be able to believe in you either.

Let us end with a quote from one of the legends of English soccer.

"Some people tell me that we professional players are soccer slaves. Well, if this is slavery, give me a life sentence" ~ *Sir Robert "Bobby" Charlton.*

(1937: former English footballer; still the all-time highest goal scorer for England and Manchester United).

End.

I sincerely wish you all the best in all your endeavors to succeed.

Mirsad Hasic

About The Author

Mirsad writes all of his books in a unique style, constantly drawing connections between his past experiences and his reader's goals.

This unique approach means that you can avoid undergoing the same injuries, frustrations, and setbacks that he himself has endured over the years.

He can't produce the results for you, but what he can do is promise that you WILL reach your goals - guaranteed – providing you follow his tips and advice exactly as he outlines them in his books.

Made in the USA
San Bernardino, CA
20 December 2015